Little Science Stars

Electricity

The Best Start in Science

By Clint Twist

ticktock

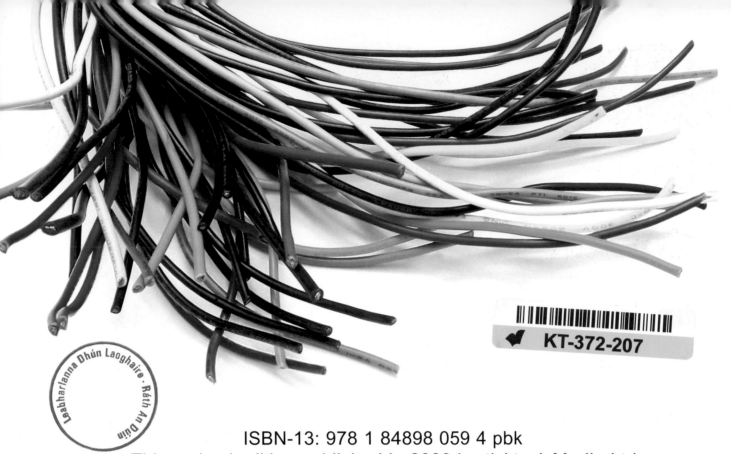

ISBN-13: 978 1 84898 059 4 pbk
This revised edition published in 2009 by *ticktock* Media Ltd

Printed in China
9 8 7 6 5 4 3 2 1

A CIP catalogue record for this book is available from the British Library.

First published in Great Britain as *Check It Out!* in 2005 by *ticktock* Media Ltd, The Old Sawmill, 103 Goods Station Road, Tunbridge Wells, Kent, TN1 2DP

Picture credits (t=top, b=bottom, c=centre, l=left, r=right, OFC=outside front cover, OBC=outside back cover):

Corbis: 17b. iStock: OFCc. Powerstock: 10c, 10b, 12t, 13, 14 all, 15 all, 16c, 16b, 17t, 20t, 21c. Shutterstock: OFCt, OFCb, 1 all, 2, 3 all, 4–5 all, 6 all, 7 all, 8 all, 9 all, 10t, 11 all, 12c, 12b, 16t, 17c, 18 all, 19 all, 21t, 21b, 22 all, 23 all, 24 all, OBC both.

Every effort has been made to trace the copyright holders and we apologize in advance for any unintentional omissions. We would be pleased to insert the appropriate acknowledgements in any subsequent edition of this publication.

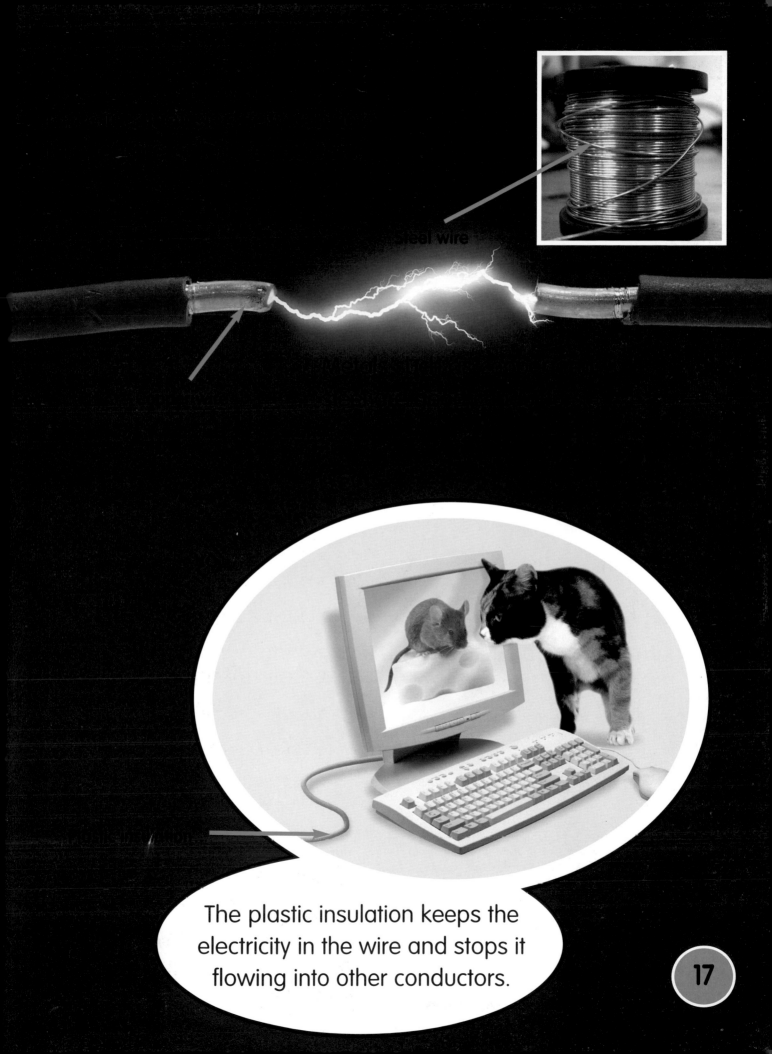

steel wire

The plastic insulation keeps the
electricity in the wire and stops it
flowing into other conductors.

How do we make electricity?

Electricity for our homes, schools, offices and factories is made at a power station.

Many power stations burn **coal** to make electricity.

Coal

This way of making electricity sends smoke and other harmful stuff up into the air. This is hurting our planet.

Power lines

Pylon

Electricity is sent down **power lines** to where it is needed. Tall towers, called **pylons**, hold up the power lines.

There are other ways to make electricity that are kinder to our planet.

Wind turbines

When the wind blows, these wind turbines turn and make electricity.

We can use solar panels to collect the Sun's energy and turn it into electricity.

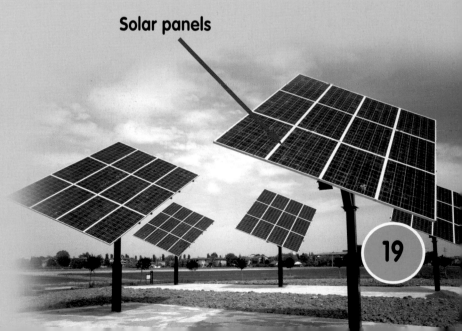

Solar panels

19

What do we need to know about electricity?

Electricity flows from the power lines through wires in our homes to electrical **sockets**.

Machines, like this fridge, are plugged into the electrical sockets.

DANGER
Do NOT poke your fingers or anything else into an electrical socket. Electricity is strong enough to kill you!

Electricity is important in our lives – let's try not to waste it!

Use energy saving light bulbs as they use 80 per cent less electricity. Like ordinary bulbs, they come in all shapes and sizes.

Don't just switch off your TV with the remote control, switch it off completely at the wall socket.

Shut down the computer when you have finished using it.

What other things can YOU do to save electricity?

21

Questions
and answers

Q How did people heat and light their homes before electricity was invented?

A They lit candles for light and burned wood to keep warm.

Q Why do light bulbs sometimes stop working?

A The tiny wire inside the bulb has burned through so the electricity can no longer flow.

Q Who invented the light bulb?

A It was invented in 1880 by an American inventor, Thomas Edison, and a British inventor named Sir Joseph Wilson Swan.

4 How Science Works (10.1-10.9)

Biology Unit 2

12 What are animals and plants built from? (11.1)

14 How do dissolved substances get into and out of cells? (11.2) and How do plants obtain the food they need to live and grow? (11.3)

18 What happens to energy and biomass at each stage in a food chain? (11.4)

22 What happens to waste material produced by plants and animals? (11.5)

23 What are enzymes and what are some of their functions? (11.6)

27 How do our bodies keep internal conditions constant? (11.7)

31 Which human characteristics show a simple pattern of inheritance? (11.8)

40 Example Questions

41 Key Words

Chemistry Unit 2

42 How do sub-atomic particles help us to understand the structure of substances? (12.1) and How do structures influence the properties and uses of substances? (12.2)

50 How much can we make and how much do we need to use? (12.3)

58 How can we control the rates of chemical reactions? (12.4)

63 Do chemical reactions always release energy? (12.5)

67 How can we use ions in solutions? (12.6)

74 Example Questions

75 Key Words

Physics Unit 2

76 How can we describe the way things move? (13.1)

80 How can we make things speed up or slow down? (13.2)

85 What happens to the movement energy when things speed up or slow down? (13.3)

87 What is momentum? (13.4)

91 What is static electricity, how can it be used and what is the connection between static electricity and electric currents? (13.5)

95 What does the current through an electrical circuit depend on? (13.6)

99 What is mains electricity and how can it be used safely? (13.7)

103 Why do we need to know the power of electrical appliances? (13.8)

105 What happens to radioactive substances when they decay? (13.9)

108 What are nuclear fission and nuclear fusion? (13.10)

110 Example Questions

111 Key Words

112 Index

113 Periodic Table

The numbers in brackets correspond to the reference numbers on the AQA GCSE Additional Science specification.

How Science Works

The new AQA GCSE Additional Science specification incorporates two types of content:

- **Science Content** (example shown opposite)
  This is all the scientific explanations and evidence that you need to be able to recall in your exams (objective tests or written exams). It is covered on pages 12–111 of the revision guide.

- **How Science Works** (example shown opposite)
  This is a set of key concepts, relevant to all areas of science. It is concerned with how scientific evidence is obtained and the effect it has on society. More specifically, it covers…

  - the relationship between scientific evidence and scientific explanations and theories
  - the practices and procedures used to collect scientific evidence
  - the reliability and validity of scientific evidence
  - the role of science in society and the impact it has on our lives
  - how decisions are made about the use of science and technology in different situations, and the factors affecting these decisions.

Because they are interlinked, your teacher will have taught the two types of content together in your science lessons. Likewise, the questions on your exam papers are likely to combine elements from both types of content, i.e. to answer them, you will need to recall the relevant scientific facts *and* draw upon your knowledge of how science works.

The key concepts from How Science Works are summarised in this section of the revision guide. You should be familiar with all of them, especially the practices and procedures used to collect scientific data (from all your practical investigations). But make sure you work through them all. Make a note if there is anything you are unsure about and then ask your teacher for clarification.

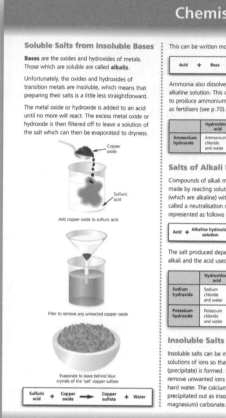

How to Use This Revision Guide

The AQA GCSE Additional Science specification includes activities for each sub-section of science content, which require you to apply your knowledge of how science works, to help develop your skills when it comes to evaluating information, developing arguments and drawing conclusions.

These activities are dealt with on the How Science Works pages (on a tinted background) throughout the revision guide. Make sure you work through them all, as questions relating to the skills, ideas and issues covered on these pages could easily come up in the exam. Bear in mind that these pages are designed to provide a starting point from which you can begin to develop your own ideas and conclusions. They are not meant to be definitive or prescriptive.

Practical tips on how to evaluate information are included in this section, on page 11.

What is the Purpose of Science?

Science attempts to explain the world we live in. The role of a scientist is to collect evidence through investigations to...

- explain phenomena (e.g. explain how and why something happens)
- solve problems.

Scientific knowledge and understanding can lead to the development of new technologies (e.g. in medicine and industry) which have a huge impact on society and the environment.

Scientific Evidence

The purpose of evidence is to provide facts which answer a specific question, and therefore support or disprove an idea or theory. In science, evidence is often based on data that has been collected by making observations and measurements.

To allow scientists to reach appropriate conclusions, evidence must be...

- **reliable**, i.e. it must be reproducible by others and therefore be trustworthy
- **valid**, i.e. it must be reliable and it must answer the question.

N.B. If data is not reliable, it cannot be valid.

To ensure scientific evidence is reliable and valid, scientists employ a range of ideas and practices which relate to...

1. **observations** – how we observe the world
2. **investigations** – designing investigations so that patterns and relationships can be identified
3. **measurements** – making measurements by selecting and using instruments effectively
4. **presenting data** – presenting and representing data
5. **conclusions** – identifying patterns and relationships and making suitable conclusions.

These five key ideas are covered in more detail on the following pages.

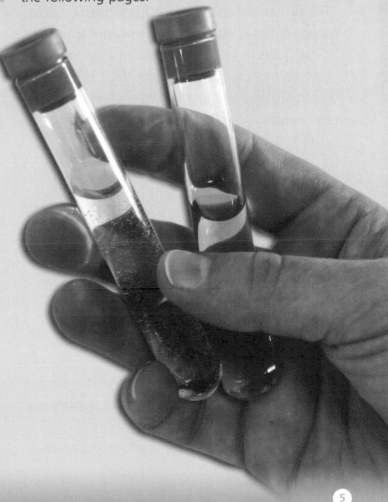

How Science Works

① Observations

Most scientific investigations begin with an observation, i.e. a scientist observes an event or phenomenon and decides to find out more about how and why it happens.

The first step is to develop a **hypothesis**, i.e. to *suggest* an explanation for the phenomenon. Hypotheses normally propose a relationship between two or more variables (factors that change). They are based on careful observations and existing scientific knowledge, and often include a bit of creative thinking.

The hypothesis is used to make a prediction, which can be tested through scientific investigation. The data collected during the investigation might support the hypothesis, show it to be untrue, or lead to the development of a new hypothesis.

Example

A biologist **observes** that freshwater shrimp are only found in certain parts of a stream.

He uses current scientific knowledge of shrimp behaviour and water flow to develop a **hypothesis**, which relates the distribution of shrimp (first variable) to the rate of water flow (second variable).

Based on this hypothesis, the biologist **predicts** that shrimp can only be found in areas of the stream where the flow rate is beneath a certain value.

The prediction is **investigated** through a survey, which looks for the presence of shrimp in different parts of the stream, representing a range of different flow rates.

The **data** shows that shrimp are only present in parts of the stream where the flow rate is below a certain value (i.e. it supports the hypothesis). However, it also shows that shrimp are not *always* present in parts of the stream where the flow rate is below this value.

As a result, the biologist realises there must be another factor affecting the distribution of shrimp. So, he **refines his hypothesis**, to relate the distribution of shrimp (first variable) to the concentration of oxygen in the water (second variable) in parts of the stream where there is a slow flow rate.

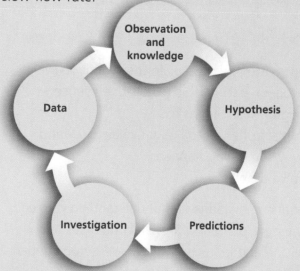

If new observations or data do not match existing explanations or theories, e.g. if unexpected behaviour is displayed, they need to be checked for reliability and validity.

In some cases it turns out that the new observations and data are valid, so existing theories and explanations have to be revised or amended. This is how scientific knowledge gradually grows and develops.

❷ Investigations

An investigation involves collecting data to try to determine whether there is a relationship between two variables. A variable is any factor that can take different values (i.e. change). In an investigation you have two variables:

- **independent variable**, which is controlled or known by the person carrying out the investigation. In the shrimp example on page 6, the independent variable is the flow rate of the water.
- **dependent variable**, which is measured each time a change is made to the independent variable, to see if it also changes. In the shrimp example on page 6, the dependent variable is the distribution of shrimp (i.e. whether shrimp are present or not).

Variables can have different types of values...

- **continuous variables** – can take any numerical values. These are usually measurements, e.g. temperature or height.
- **discrete variables** – can only take whole-number values. These are usually quantities, e.g. the number of shrimp in a population.
- **ordered variables** – have relative values, e.g. small, medium or large.
- **categoric variables** – have a limited number of specific values, e.g. the different breeds of dog: dalmatian, cocker spaniel, labrador etc.

Numerical values tend to be more powerful and informative than ordered variables and categoric variables.

An investigation tries to establish whether an observed link between two variables is...

- **causal** – a change in one variable causes a change in the other, e.g. in a chemical reaction the rate of reaction (dependent variable) increases when the temperature of the reactants (independent variable) is increased
- **due to association** – the changes in the two variables are linked by a third variable, e.g. a link between the change in pH of a stream (first variable) and a change in the number of different species found in the stream (second variable), may be the effect of a change in the concentration of atmospheric pollutants (third variable)
- **due to chance** – the change in the two variables is unrelated; it is coincidental, e.g. in the 1940s the number of deaths due to lung cancer increased as did the amount of tar being used in road construction, however, one *did not* cause the other.

How Science Works

Fair Test

A fair test is one in which the only factor that can affect the dependent variable is the independent variable. Any other variables (outside variables) that could influence the results are kept the same.

This is a lot easier in the laboratory than in the field, where conditions (e.g. weather) cannot always be physically controlled. The impact of outside variables, like the weather, has to be reduced by ensuring all measurements are affected by the variable in the same way. For example, if you were investigating the effect of different fertilisers on the growth of tomato plants, all the plants would need to be grown in a place where they were subject to the same weather conditions.

If a survey is used to collect data, the impact of outside variables can be reduced by ensuring that the individuals in the sample are closely matched. For example, if you were investigating the effect of smoking on life expectancy, the individuals in the sample would all need to have a similar diet and lifestyle to ensure that those variables do not affect the results.

Control groups are often used in biological research. For example, in some drugs trials, a placebo (a dummy pill containing no medicine) is given to one group of volunteers – the control group – and the drug is given to another. By comparing the two groups, scientists can establish whether the drug (the independent variable) is the only variable affecting the volunteers and, therefore, whether it is a fair test.

Accuracy and Precision

In an investigation, the mean (average) of a set of repeated measurements is often calculated to overcome small variations and get a best estimate of the true value. Increasing the number of measurements taken will improve the accuracy and the reliability of their mean.

$$\text{Mean} = \frac{\text{Sum of all measurements}}{\text{Number of measurements}}$$

The purpose of an investigation will determine how accurate the data collected needs to be. For example, measures of blood alcohol levels must be accurate enough to determine whether a person is legally fit to drive.

The data collected must also be precise enough to form a valid conclusion, i.e. it should provide clear evidence for or against the hypothesis.

How Science Works

③ Measurements

Even if all outside variables have been controlled, there are certain factors that could still affect the reliability and validity of any measurements made:

- **the accuracy of the instruments used** – The accuracy of a measuring instrument will depend on how accurately it has been calibrated. Expensive equipment is likely to be more accurately calibrated.
- **the sensitivity of the instruments used** – The sensitivity of an instrument is determined by the smallest change in value it can detect. For example, bathroom scales are not sensitive enough to detect the changes in weight of a small baby, whereas the scales used by a midwife to monitor growth are.
- **human error** – When making measurements, random errors can occur due to a lapse in concentration, and systematic (repeated) errors can occur if the instrument has not been calibrated properly or is repeatedly misused.

Any anomalous (irregular) values, e.g. values that fall well outside the range (the spread) of the other measurements, need to be examined to try to determine the cause. If they have been caused by an equipment failure or human error, it is common practice to ignore such values and discount them from any following calculations.

> **Range** **=** **Maximum value** **−** **Minimum value**

④ Presenting Data

Data is often presented in a format that makes the patterns more evident. This makes it easier to see the relationship between two variables. The relationship between variables can be linear (positive or negative) or directly proportional.

Clear presentation of data also makes it easier to identify any anomalous values.

The type of chart or graph used to present data will depend on the type of variable involved.

Tables organise data (patterns and anomalies in the data are not always obvious).

Height (cm)	127	165	149	147	155	161	154	138	145
Shoe size	5	8	5	6	5	5	6	4	5

Bar charts are used to display data when the independent variable is categoric or discrete and the dependent variable is continuous.

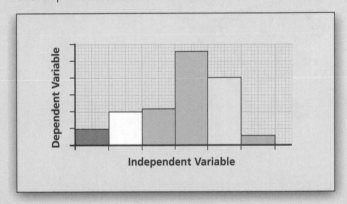

Line graphs are used to display data when both variables are continuous.

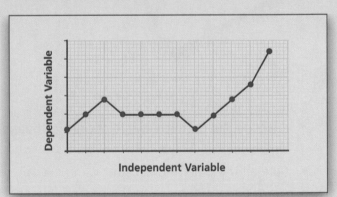

Scattergrams (or scatter diagrams) are used to show the underlying relationship between two variables. This can be made clearer by including a line of best fit.

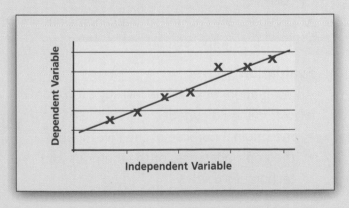

How Science Works

⑤ Conclusions

Conclusions should...
- describe the patterns and relationships between variables
- take all the data into account
- make direct reference to the original hypothesis / prediction.

Conclusions should not...
- be influenced by anything other than the data collected
- disregard any data (other than anomalous values)
- include any speculation.

Evaluation

An evaluation looks at the investigation as a whole. It should consider...
- the original purpose of the investigation
- the appropriateness of the methods and techniques used

- the reliability and validity of the data
- the validity of the conclusions (e.g. whether the original purpose was achieved).

The reliability of an investigation can be increased by...
- looking at relevant data from secondary sources
- using an alternative method to check results
- ensuring that the results can be reproduced by others.

Science and Society

Scientific understanding can lead to technological developments, which can be exploited by different groups of people for different reasons. For example, the successful development of a new drug benefits the drugs company financially and improves the quality of life for patients.

The applications of scientific and technological developments can raise certain issues. An issue is an important question that is in dispute and needs to be settled. Decisions made by individuals and society about these issues may not be based on scientific evidence alone.

Social issues are concerned with the impact on the human population of a community, city, country, or even the world.

Economic issues are concerned with money and related factors like employment and the distribution of resources. There is often an overlap between social and economic issues.

Environmental issues are concerned with the impact on the planet; its natural ecosystems and resources.

Ethical issues are concerned with what is morally right and wrong, i.e. they require a value judgement to be made about what is acceptable. As society is underpinned by a common belief system, there are certain actions that can never be justified. However, because the views of individuals are influenced by lots of different factors (e.g. faith and personal experience) there are also lots of grey areas.

How Science Works

Evaluating Information

It is important that you can evaluate information relating to social-scientific issues. You could be asked to do this in the exam, but it will also help you make informed decisions in life (e.g. decide whether or not to have a particular vaccination or become involved in a local recycling campaign).

When you are asked to **evaluate** information, start by making a list of the pluses and the minuses. Then work through the two lists, and for each point consider how this might impact on society. Remember, **PMI** – pluses, minuses, impact on society.

You also need to be sure that the source of information is reliable and credible. Here are some important factors to consider:

- **opinion**
  Opinions are personal viewpoints. Opinions which are backed up by valid and reliable evidence carry far more weight than those based on non-scientific ideas (e.g. hearsay or urban myths).

- **bias**
  Information is biased if it does not provide a balanced account; it favours a particular viewpoint. Biased information might include incomplete evidence or try to influence how you interpret the evidence. For example, a drugs company might highlight the benefits of their drugs but downplay the side effects in order to increase sales.

- **weight of evidence**
  Scientific evidence can be given undue weight or dismissed too lightly due to...
  - political significance, e.g. evidence that is likely to provoke an extreme and negative reaction from the public might be downplayed
  - status (academic or professional status, experience, authority and reputation), e.g. evidence is likely to be given more weight if it comes from someone who is a recognised expert in that particular field.

Limitations of Science

Science can help us in lots of ways but it cannot supply all the answers. We are still finding out about things and developing our scientific knowledge. There are some questions that we cannot answer, maybe because we do not have enough reliable and valid evidence.

There are some questions that science cannot answer at all. These tend to be questions relating to ethical issues, where beliefs and opinions are important, or to situations where we cannot collect reliable and valid scientific evidence. In other words, science can often tell us whether something *can* be done and *how* it can be done, but it cannot tell us whether it *should* be done.

Biology Unit 2

What are animals and plants built from?

All living organisms are made up of cells. The structure of each cell depends on its function. To understand this, you need to know...

- the different parts of cells, and the functions of these parts
- how chemical reactions are controlled in cells
- how cells are adapted to carry out particular functions.

Typical Plant and Animal Cells

All living organisms are made up of cells. The structures of different types of cells are related to their functions.

A palisade cell from a leaf

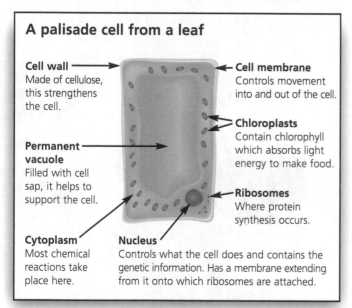

Cell wall
Made of cellulose, this strengthens the cell.

Cell membrane
Controls movement into and out of the cell.

Chloroplasts
Contain chlorophyll which absorbs light energy to make food.

Permanent vacuole
Filled with cell sap, it helps to support the cell.

Ribosomes
Where protein synthesis occurs.

Cytoplasm
Most chemical reactions take place here.

Nucleus
Controls what the cell does and contains the genetic information. Has a membrane extending from it onto which ribosomes are attached.

A cheek cell from a human

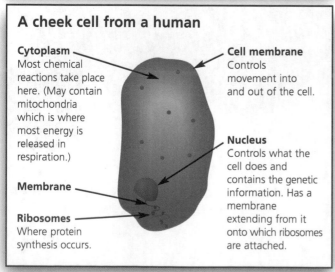

Cytoplasm
Most chemical reactions take place here. (May contain mitochondria which is where most energy is released in respiration.)

Cell membrane
Controls movement into and out of the cell.

Membrane

Nucleus
Controls what the cell does and contains the genetic information. Has a membrane extending from it onto which ribosomes are attached.

Ribosomes
Where protein synthesis occurs.

Some cells are specialised to do a particular job.

Root hair cells have a tiny hair-like structure which increases the surface area of the cell enabling it to absorb water and ions more efficiently.	
Palisade cells are column-shaped cells on the upper surface of the leaf. They are packed with chloroplasts for photosynthesis.	
Xylem cells are long, thin, hollow cells that contain no cytoplasm (they are actually dead!). They transport water through the stem and root.	
Nerve cells (neurones) have long slender axons which can carry nerve impulses over distances as long as one metre.	
The **ovum** or **egg cell** is much larger than other cells so that it can carry massive food reserves for the developing embryo.	
The **sperm cell** is the most mobile cell because of its tail. It has to travel from the vagina to the ovum.	
Red blood cells have no nucleus so that they can be packed full of haemoglobin in order to carry lots of oxygen.	Cross section
White blood cells can change their shape in order to engulf and destroy microbes which have invaded the body.	

Most cells are made up of water containing dissolved substances. These substances are usually in the process of being made into something the cell needs. This involves chemical reactions controlled by enzymes. Enzymes are found in cytoplasm and in all **mitochondria** (which produce the cell's energy).

You need to be able to relate the structure of different types of cells to their function in a tissue or an organ.

Example

The Lonsdale News, Saturday, June 24, 2006   14

environment**watch**

Deadly Fungus Threatens Frogs

The alarmingly extensive spread of a deadly fungus throughout America is causing great concern. Scientists have reported that hundreds of thousands of the much-loved golden frog, a national emblem, are dying from the effects of the fungus.

The fungus is thought to affect other amphibians as well and scientists are currently planning investigations to find out how many other species are being affected, and to what extent.

Ask Greenfingers

Dear Greenfingers,
No matter what I put into my soil – I've tried expensive nutrients and fertilisers etc. – my plants always seem to be droopy in the summer. Why does this keep happening and what can I do to prevent it this year?
Yours, Concerned of Colchester

Dear Concerned,
Sometimes, no matter how rich in nutrients your soil is, or what fertiliser you use, you can end up with droopy plants. The fact that this usually happens in the summer suggests that your plants are suffering from a lack of water. They get dehydrated just like we do, so what they need is a good watering. Ideally you should try to water your plants every day. It is best to wait until early evening to water your plants, when the heat of the sun is less powerful. I hope you have better luck with your plants this year!

Why are the frogs dying?

Frogs' skin is made of a layer of cells which have permeable cell walls. These permeable cell walls allow the passage of water and gases into the frog's blood when it is resting. This means that a frog can breathe through its skin as well as taking in water simply by jumping into a pond or sitting in a puddle.

If the skin cells are covered by an impermeable layer, such as the fungus mentioned in the article above, the cells get blocked up, which makes the exchange of liquids and gases extremely difficult and eventually the frog will die.

Why do plants droop when they do not have enough water?

Water is transported through the root and stem of a plant via long thin cells, which do not have end walls, that make up the xylem. The walls of these cells are strengthened by rings of lignin (a rigid deposit), which enable them to withstand the pressure of water. The water pressure within the xylem makes the plant turgid and strong. If there is not enough water in the cells, the cell walls become limp and flaccid and the plant droops.

Biology Unit 2

11.2 and 11.3

How do dissolved substances get into and out of cells?

Dissolved substances pass through the cell membranes to get into and out of the cells. To understand this, you need to know…
- what diffusion is
- what osmosis is
- what causes osmosis.

How do plants obtain the food they need to live and grow?

Green plants make their own food using air, soil and energy from the sun. To understand this, you need to know…
- how photosynthesis works and the factors that can slow it down
- how the glucose produced during photosynthesis is used
- what plants need to ensure healthy growth
- what happens when plants are deficient in mineral ions.

Amoeba – a single-celled organism (not to scale)

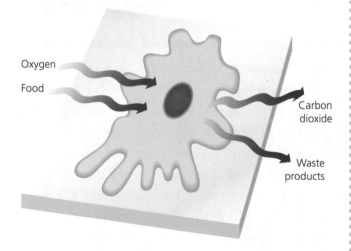

Oxygen
Food
Carbon dioxide
Waste products

Oxygen, carbon dioxide, food and waste products, along with simple sugars and ions, pass easily through cell membranes.

Dissolved substances can move into and out of cells by diffusion and osmosis.

Diffusion

Because cells are living things, they constantly have to replace substances which are used up (e.g. food and oxygen) and remove other substances which would otherwise accumulate (e.g. carbon dioxide and waste products).

Even simple, single-celled animals, like the amoeba (below left), need to do this. This can take place automatically, without the need for energy, in a process called **diffusion**.

Diffusion is the spreading of the particles of a gas, or of any substance in solution, which results in a net movement from a region where they are at a higher concentration to a region where they are at a lower concentration. For example, oxygen required for respiration passes through all membranes by diffusion.

The greater the difference in concentration, the faster the rate of diffusion. So in the example of oxygen and the amoeba, there is lots of oxygen outside the amoeba but much less inside, because it is being used up in respiration. This results in the rapid diffusion of oxygen into the amoeba through the cell membrane.

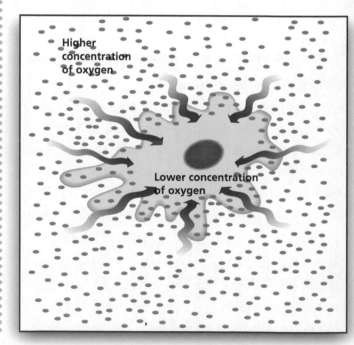

Higher concentration of oxygen

Lower concentration of oxygen

Osmosis

Osmosis is the movement of water from a dilute solution (e.g. with a high water to solute ratio) to a more concentrated solution (e.g. with a low water to solute ratio) through a partially permeable membrane. The membrane allows the water molecules through but not the solute molecules because they are too large.

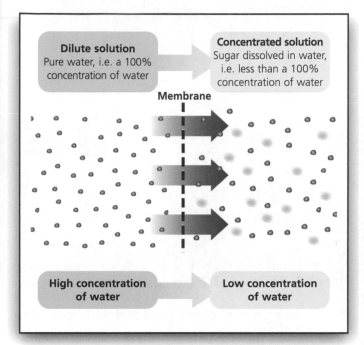

Dilute solution Pure water, i.e. a 100% concentration of water	→	**Concentrated solution** Sugar dissolved in water, i.e. less than a 100% concentration of water

Membrane

High concentration of water	→	**Low concentration of water**

The effect of osmosis is to gradually dilute the solution. This is what happens at root hair cells, where water moves from the soil into the cell by osmosis, along a concentration gradient.

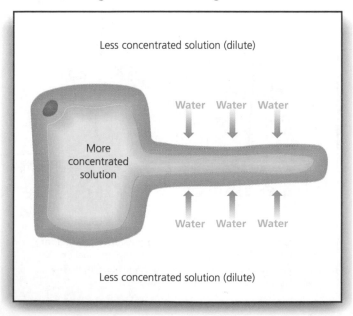

Less concentrated solution (dilute)

Water   Water   Water

More concentrated solution

Water   Water   Water

Less concentrated solution (dilute)

Making Food using Energy from the Sun

Green plants don't absorb food from the soil. They make their own using sunlight. This is called **photosynthesis**. It occurs in the cells of green plants, which are exposed to light.

Four things are needed...
*   light from the Sun
*   carbon dioxide diffused from the air
*   water from the soil
*   chlorophyll in the leaves.

Two things are produced...
*   glucose – for biomass and energy
*   oxygen – released into the atmosphere as a by-product.

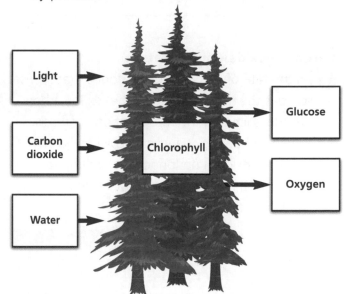

Light → Chlorophyll → Glucose

Carbon dioxide →

Water → → Oxygen

The word equation for photosynthesis is...

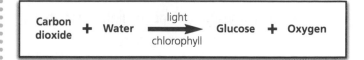

$$\text{Carbon dioxide} + \text{Water} \xrightarrow[\text{chlorophyll}]{\text{light}} \text{Glucose} + \text{Oxygen}$$

Light energy is absorbed by green chlorophyll (in chloroplasts in some plant cells).

Some of the glucose produced in photosynthesis is used immediately by the plant to provide energy via respiration. However, much of the glucose is converted into insoluble starch which is stored in the stem, leaves or roots.

Biology Unit 2

Factors Affecting Photosynthesis

Temperature, carbon dioxide concentration and light intensity interact to limit the rate of photosynthesis. Any one of them, at a particular time, may be the limiting factor.

Temperature

1 As the temperature rises so does the rate of photosynthesis. This means temperature is limiting the rate of photosynthesis.

2 As the temperature approaches 45°C, the enzymes controlling photosynthesis start to be destroyed and the rate of photosynthesis drops to zero.

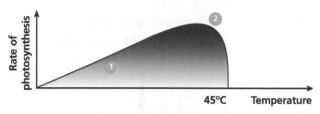

Carbon Dioxide Concentration

1 As the rate of carbon dioxide concentration rises so does the rate of photosynthesis. So carbon dioxide is limiting the rate of photosynthesis.

2 Rise in carbon dioxide levels now has no effect. Carbon dioxide is no longer the limiting factor. Light or temperature must now be the limiting factor.

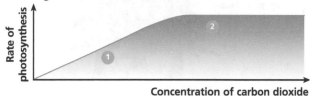

Light Intensity

1 As the light intensity increases so does the rate of photosynthesis. This means light intensity is limiting the rate of photosynthesis.

2 Rise in light intensity now has no effect. Light intensity is no longer the limiting factor. Carbon dioxide or temperature must now be the limiting factor.

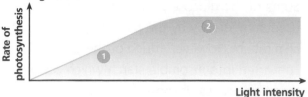

Photosynthesis, and therefore growth, can be controlled when these factors are controlled. For example, a greenhouse can be modified to...
- increase temperature (up to about 40°C)
- increase CO_2 levels
- increase light intensity.

This will result in plants growing more quickly and becoming bigger and stronger.

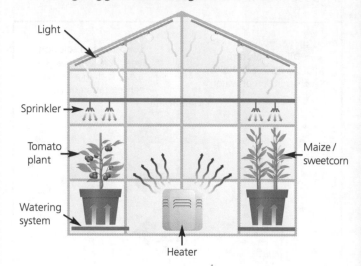

Plant Mineral Requirements

For healthy growth, plants need mineral ions which they absorb from soil through their roots, including nitrates and magnesium.

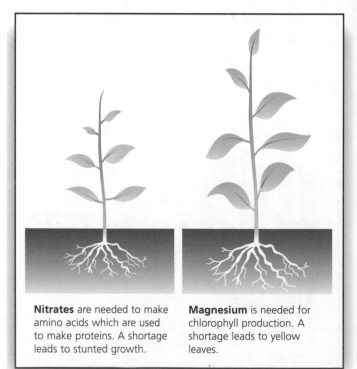

Nitrates are needed to make amino acids which are used to make proteins. A shortage leads to stunted growth.

Magnesium is needed for chlorophyll production. A shortage leads to yellow leaves.

How Science Works

You need to be able to interpret data showing how factors affect the rate of photosynthesis, and **evaluate the benefits of artificially manipulating the environment in which plants are grown.**

Example

Charlie decided to investigate the benefits of growing lettuces in artificially controlled conditions.

He used a fossil burner to investigate what effects varying the amount of carbon dioxide in the air would have on his lettuces and used weight as an indicator of growth and therefore the rate of photosynthesis.

He divided 50 lettuces into five groups that weighed the same overall. He then adjusted the level of carbon dioxide in each group's air (the independent variable), but made sure that the temperature and the amount of light and water each group received was the same (controlled variables). After eight weeks, he weighed each group again (dependent variable). The graph above shows his results.

Conclusion

The graph shows that the more carbon dioxide in the air, the greater the mass of the lettuces. Carbon dioxide aids photosynthesis, which is why the plants that had more carbon dioxide in the air grew more than those with a lower percentage of carbon dioxide. However, it is also important to notice that the graph levels off between 4% and 5%, which would suggest that this is the optimum percentage of carbon dioxide needed for photosynthesis. Increasing the levels of carbon dioxide present in the air beyond this would not increase the rate of photosynthesis and therefore would not affect the weight of the lettuce.

Advantage of Controlling Carbon Dioxide	Disadvantages of Controlling Carbon Dioxide
• Larger average mass of lettuces produced.	• Cost of carbon dioxide machine. • Need to monitor the levels of carbon dioxide. • Other factors could be involved that have not been taken into consideration.

Biology Unit 2

What happens to energy and biomass at each stage in a food chain?

The relative amount of energy and biomass decreases at each stage in a food chain. To understand this, you need to know...

- what pyramids of biomass show
- how the Sun provides energy for many living organisms
- the ways in which energy and biomass are reduced at each stage in the food chain
- how the efficiency of food production in the food chain can be improved.

Food Chains

Radiation from the Sun is the source of energy for all communities of living organisms.

In green plants, photosynthesis captures a small fraction of the solar energy which reaches them. This energy is stored in the substances which make up the cells of the plant and can be passed onto organisms which eat the plant. This transfer of energy can be represented by a food chain.

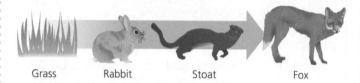

Grass   Rabbit   Stoat   Fox

Pyramids of Biomass

The mass of living material (**biomass**) at each stage of a food chain is less than it was at the previous stage. The biomass at each stage can be drawn to scale and shown as a pyramid of biomass.

3rd (tertiary) consumer

2nd (secondary) consumer

1st (primary) consumer

Producer

FLOW OF ENERGY

Transfer of Energy and Biomass

Biomass and energy are lost at every stage of a food chain because materials and energy are lost in an organism's faeces (waste).

Energy released through respiration is used up in movement and lost as heat energy.

This is particularly true in warm-blooded animals (birds and mammals), whose bodies must be kept at a constant temperature, higher than their surroundings.

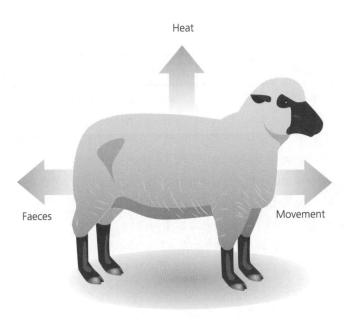

In the pyramid on page 18, the fox gets the last tiny bit of energy and biomass that is left.

Only a fraction of the Sun's energy is captured by the producers. Much of the biomass remains in the root system and so doesn't get eaten.

Rabbits run, mate, excrete, generate heat and pass on only a tenth of the energy they get from grass. A lot of biomass is lost in droppings (faeces).

Stoats run, mate, excrete, generate heat and pass on only a tenth of the energy they get from the rabbits. A lot of biomass is lost as faeces.

Foxes, as third consumers, only receive a small amount of the energy captured by the grass at the bottom of the pyramid.

Improving the Efficiency of Food Production

Since the loss of energy and biomass is due mainly to heat loss, waste and movement, it follows that we can improve the efficiency of food production by reducing the number of stages in a food chain

…is not as efficient as…

or by limiting an animal's movement, and controlling its temperature.

More of the food eaten by the animal is then converted into biomass because less energy is lost through heat and movement.

However, many people feel that this way of rearing animals is unacceptable.

How Science Works

You need to be able to interpret pyramids of biomass and construct them from appropriate information.

Example

Carp
(tertiary consumer)

Pond snail
(secondary consumer)

Water beetle
(primary consumer)

Phytoplankton
(producer)

By looking at the pyramid of biomass above, we can see that it represents a pond community. It shows the relative biomass of four species that live in the pond and it also shows us what eats what in the food chain.

We can see that the producer is phytoplankton (a plant). This provides food and energy for the water beetles, which are eaten by pond snails, which in turn are consumed by carp. We can also see that the biomass of living material reduces as you go further up the pyramid (more levels of consumers). This is because biomass is lost as waste products, e.g. faeces and carbon dioxide.

The table opposite provides details of other organisms in the pond.

Species	Producer / Feeds On
Phytoplankton	Producer
Elodea (water plant)	Producer
Algae	Producer
Water beetle	Feeds on water plants
Carp	Feeds on insect larvae and snails
Pond snail	Feeds on water plants and small insects
Mosquito larvae	Feeds on insect algae and protozoa
Leech	Feeds on pond snails
Stickleback	Feeds on insect larvae and leeches

To construct a pyramid of biomass from this information there are a few basic rules to follow:

- it will be pyramid shaped!
- biomass is the mass of living material
- the producers are placed at the bottom
- the pyramid represents the total biomass at each stage, not the number of organisms.

Stickleback
(tertiary consumer)

Leech
(secondary consumer)

Pond snail
(primary consumer)

Elodea
(producer)

You need to be able to evaluate the positive and negative effects of managing food production and distribution, and recognise that practical solutions to human needs may require compromise between competing priorities.

Example

Farming Gazette   *June 2006*

Union Votes to Ban Battery Cages

In 1999, the European Commission proposed that the floor size of battery hen cages should be increased to a minimum of 800cm^2 (from 450cm^2). However, members of the European Parliament went even further and voted by a majority of two to one to ban battery hen cages altogether. They agreed that the ban should be enforced throughout Europe, as of 2009.

Some 93% of all eggs in the EU are produced by battery hens, so this new legislation will create a great upheaval in the European egg market.

Current Conditions
There are up to 30 million chickens in the UK; 85% live in 'battery farms' where they are kept in sheds that contain over 20,000 birds. By restricting the movement of the birds, the energy usually lost in movement is converted into meat and the chickens get bigger more quickly, which means they can be sold for meat at an earlier age. The chickens are also exposed to artificial sunrise and sunset so that egg production is increased.

A European scientific report stated that chickens kept in confined spaces can have serious health problems, including hock burn (brown marks on their legs), and pressure on the heart and legs. About 100,000 chickens die each day.

Ideal Conditions
'Free range' chickens are housed in sheds with perches but they have access to the outside during the day. However, 'free range' chickens and their eggs could be up to 25% more expensive than battery hens and their eggs.

Farmers' Concerns
Poultry farmers are worried that these changes to the industry could result in them losing money. Countries outside the EU could provide cheap imports into UK supermarkets which could be sold cheaper than UK eggs and chicken.

The Solution
In Britain, scientists were asked to provide guidelines to enable Britain to comply with the European legislation. They came up with the 'Battery Cage Rule': all battery cages are to be converted to 'enriched cages' by 2007 (enriched cages provide at least 750cm^2 floor space per bird) and all battery hen farms are to be replaced by free range and barn systems by 2012. The time delay, and the rule on 'enriched cages', was agreed in order to give farmers time to adapt their farms in order to comply with the new legislation.

The suggestion is also that imports of eggs and chickens should come only from countries with the same standards of housing hens as the EU. This would prevent UK poultry farmers losing out to cheap imports from outside the EU.

This is an example of a practical solution to human needs where there is a compromise between competing priorities.

Advantages of Battery Farming
• Cheap chicken and eggs available.
• Poultry farmers can own many chickens and therefore earn a good living.
• Do not need lots of space.
• Limiting movement increases size quicker.

Disadvantages of Battery Farming
• Chickens are kept in poor conditions.
• Many chickens die before they can be sold.
• Many chickens suffer health problems.

Biology Unit 2

11.5

What happens to the waste material produced by plants and animals?

Microbes help to decompose waste material from animals and plants. It is then used by plants as a source of nutrients. To understand this, you need to know…

- how the environment recycles waste material
- how microorganisms break down materials
- how the carbon cycle works, and its effects.

Recycling the Materials of Life

Living things remove materials from the environment for growth and other processes, but when the organisms die or excrete waste, these materials are returned to the environment.

The key to all this is the **microorganisms** which break down the waste and the dead bodies. This decay process releases substances used by plants for growth.

Microorganisms digest materials faster in warm, moist conditions where there is plenty of oxygen.

Humans also deliberately use microorganisms in…

- sewage works to break down human waste
- compost heaps to break down plant material waste.

The Carbon Cycle

In a stable community, the processes which remove materials are balanced by processes which return materials. This constant recycling of carbon is called the **Carbon Cycle**.

1. CO₂ is removed from the atmosphere by green plants to produce glucose by photosynthesis. Some is returned to the atmosphere by the plants during respiration.

2. The carbon obtained by photosynthesis is used to make carbohydrates, fats and proteins in plants. When the plants are eaten by animals this carbon becomes carbohydrates, fats and proteins in animals.

3. Animals respire releasing CO₂ into the atmosphere.

4. When plants and animals die, other animals and microorganisms feed on their bodies causing them to break down.

5. As the detritus feeders and microorganisms eat the dead plants and animals, they respire releasing CO₂ into the atmosphere.

11.6

What are enzymes and what are some of their functions?

Enzymes are produced by living cells. They are biological catalysts that have many functions inside and outside cells. To understand this, you need to know…

- what enzymes are, what they consist of, and what they do
- what processes they catalyse
- how energy released during aerobic respiration is used
- what the functions of digestive enzymes are
- how enzymes are used in the home and in industry.

Enzymes

Enzymes are biological catalysts; they increase the rate of chemical reactions in an organism.

Enzymes are protein molecules made up of long chains of **amino acids**.

A protein molecule made up of amino acids

These are folded into a 3-D shape which lets other molecules fit into the enzyme.

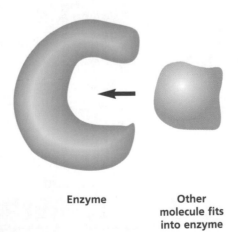

Enzyme   Other molecule fits into enzyme

Different enzymes work best at certain temperatures and pH levels.

High temperatures destroy most enzymes' special shape. This is why it's dangerous for a human's body temperature to go much above 37°C.

Enzyme destroyed by heat

Heat

Inside Living Cells

Enzymes in living cells **catalyse** (speed up) processes such as respiration, protein synthesis and photosynthesis.

The energy released during respiration is used to…
- build larger **molecules** using smaller ones
- enable **muscles** to contract (in animals)
- **maintain a constant temperature** (in mammals and birds) in colder surroundings
- **make proteins** in plants from amino acids (made from sugars and nitrates).

N.B. *They all begin with M, so remember the four 'Ms'.*

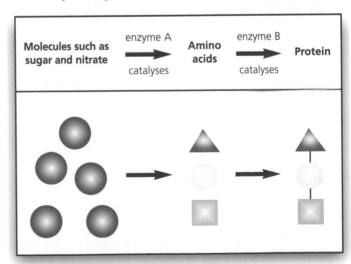

Biology Unit 2

Aerobic Respiration

Aerobic respiration releases energy through the breakdown of glucose molecules, by combining them with oxygen inside living cells. (The energy is actually contained inside the glucose molecule. Aerobic respiration mostly takes place inside mitochondria.)

The written equation for aerobic respiration is...

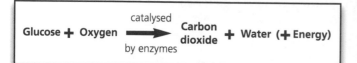

Glucose + Oxygen → Carbon dioxide + Water (+ Energy)
(catalysed by enzymes)

Outside Living Cells

Digestive enzymes are produced by specialised cells in glands in the digestive system. The enzymes pass out of the cells into the digestive system where they come into contact with food molecules.

The enzymes then catalyse the breakdown of large molecules into smaller molecules.

Three enzymes – protease, lipase and amylase – are produced in four separate regions of the digestive system. They digest proteins, fats and carbohydrates to produce smaller molecules which can be absorbed.

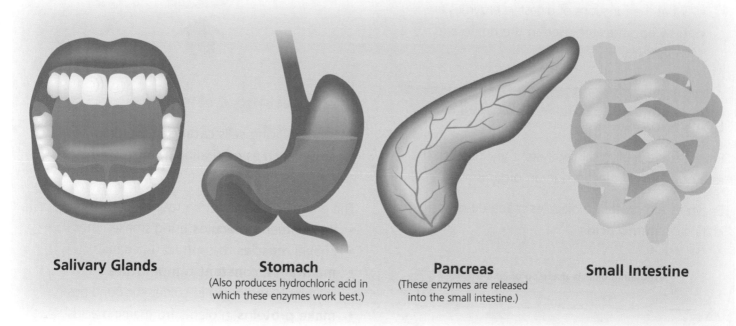

Salivary Glands

Stomach
(Also produces hydrochloric acid in which these enzymes work best.)

Pancreas
(These enzymes are released into the small intestine.)

Small Intestine

	Enzyme	What it digests	Molecules produced
Salivary glands	Amylase	Starch	Sugars
Stomach	Protease	Proteins	Amino acids
Pancreas	Amylase	Starch	Sugars
Pancreas	Protease	Proteins	Amino acids
Pancreas	Lipase	Lipids (fats and oils)	Fatty acids and glycerol
Small intestine	Amylase	Starch	Sugars
Small intestine	Protease	Proteins	Amino acids
Small intestine	Lipase	Lipids (fats and oils)	Fatty acids and glycerol

The Function of Bile

Bile is produced in the liver and then stored in the **gall bladder** before being released into the small intestine. Bile has two functions:

1. It neutralises the acid, which is added to food in the stomach, to produce alkaline conditions in which the enzymes of the small intestine work best.

2. It emulsifies fats, i.e. it breaks down large drops of fat into small droplets to increase their surface area. This enables the lipase enzymes to work much faster.

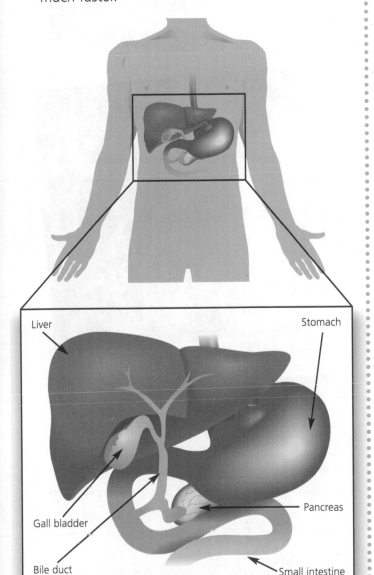

Liver

Stomach

Gall bladder

Pancreas

Bile duct

Small intestine

Globules of fat → bile → Droplets of fat

Use of Enzymes in the Home and Industry

Some microorganisms produce enzymes which can be used to our benefit both in the home and in industry.

In the Home

Biological detergents may contain...

- protein-digesting (protease) enzymes to break down blood and food stains, for example
- fat-digesting (lipase) enzymes to break down oil and grease stains.

In Industry

- Proteases are used to pre-digest protein in baby foods.
- Carbohydrases are used to convert starch into sugar syrup.
- Isomerase converts glucose syrup into fructose syrup, which is even sweeter. It can be used in smaller quantities which makes it ideal for use in slimming foods.

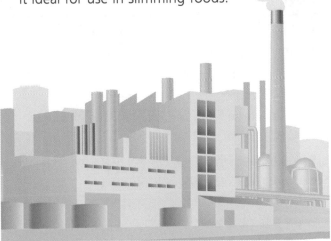

How Science Works

You need to be able to evaluate the advantages and disadvantages of using enzymes in home and industry.

If you bite into an apple and leave it for a few minutes it will turn brown. The reason behind this is the unlocking of enzymes inside the cells, which catalyse a chemical reaction with the air. This results in the flesh of the fruit turning brown.

Humans have used enzymes for thousands of years in the production of food and drink, but the use of enzymes in industry is fairly new.

Enzymes are biological catalysts; they increase the rate of a reaction without harming the cells of the living organism. These enzymes are taken from microorganisms which can be grown easily, and used over and over again. Many industries rely upon enzymes to speed up reactions that would normally require high temperatures or high pressure to proceed. These enzymes are often made in a fermenter, which may prove to be expensive.

However, without enzymes the reaction either would not happen or would take a long time to produce the commercial product. Some of the areas we use enzymes in are...

- biological detergents to remove protein stains (but some people develop skin allergies to them)
- medicine, for example, drug manufacture and glucose sensors for diabetics
- leather industry to soften hides and remove hair
- making the soft centre in sweets (the sweet is injected with an enzyme to break down the sugar inside).

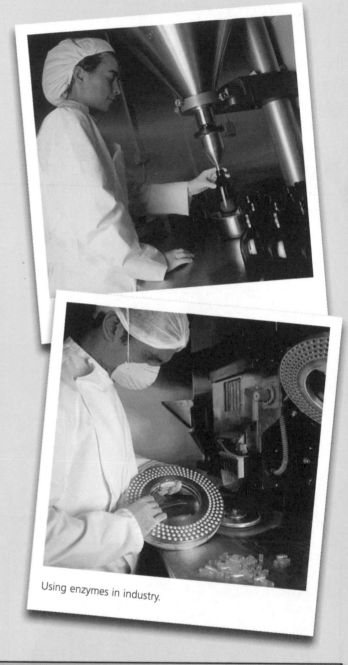

Using enzymes in industry.

Advantages	Disadvantages
• Can be used over and over again. • Speeds up reactions. • Products are made without the need for high temperatures so they are energy saving. • Many come from microorganisms which can be easily grown. • Many have been tried and tested for hundreds of years. • Have many varied applications. • Drugs for the medical industry can be made easily on a large scale so world health is improved.	• Some people are allergic to them. • Often need to be made in a large vessel called a fermenter which can be costly. • Some people don't like the idea of using microorganisms in food. • Are water soluble, so can be difficult to reclaim from a liquid.

11.7

How do our bodies keep internal conditions constant?

The body's internal environment stays constant by removing waste products regularly. To understand this you need to know...
- what waste products need to be removed, and how they are removed
- which internal body conditions need to be controlled and how the body controls them
- what happens when the body's water or ion content is wrong
- what happens when the core temperature is too high or too low
- what diabetes is and what causes it.

Controlling Conditions

The water content, ion content, temperature and blood sugar levels of the human body have to be controlled so that it can function properly.

Water and Ion Content

Water and ions enter the body through food and drink. If the water or ion content of the body is wrong, too much water may move into or out of the cells by osmosis, causing damage.

Blood Glucose Concentration

Blood glucose concentration is monitored and controlled by the pancreas which secretes the hormone insulin.

Insulin converts glucose into insoluble glycogen and lowers blood glucose (i.e. insulin allows glucose to move from the blood into the cells).

The level of insulin in the pancreas affects what happens in the liver. The pancreas continually monitors the body's blood sugar levels and adjusts the amount of insulin released to keep the body's blood sugar levels as close to normal as possible.

If the blood glucose concentration is too high...

the pancreas releases insulin.

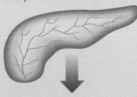

Glucose from the blood is then converted to insoluble glycogen in the liver...

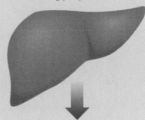

and is removed from the blood.

The blood glucose concentration returns to normal.

If the pancreas does not produce enough insulin, a person's blood glucose concentration may rise to a fatally high level. This is a condition called **diabetes**, which is treated by...
- careful attention to diet
- injecting insulin into the blood.

Biology Unit 2

Body Temperature

Body temperature should be kept at around 37°C because this is the ideal temperature for enzymes. It is controlled by the nervous system.

Monitoring and control is performed by the thermoregulatory centre in the brain, which has receptors that are sensitive to the temperature of blood flowing through it. There are also temperature receptors in the skin, which provide information about skin temperature. Sweating helps to cool the body. More water is lost when it is hot, and more water has to be taken in as food or drink to balance this.

Removing Waste Products

Humans need to remove waste products from their body to keep their internal environment relatively constant. Two of these waste products are carbon dioxide and urea.

- Carbon dioxide is produced by respiration and is removed via the lungs during exhalation.
- Urea is produced by the liver when it breaks down amino acids, and is removed by the kidneys and transferred to the bladder before it is released.

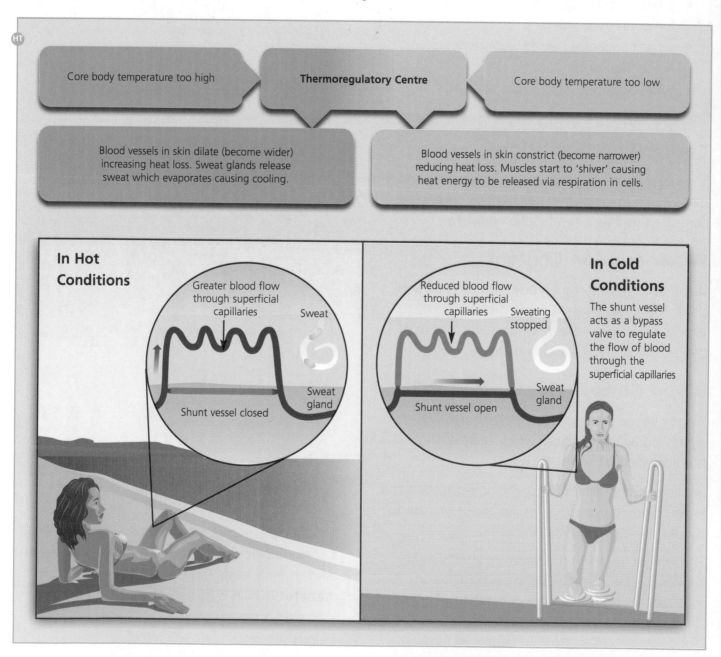

HT

Core body temperature too high

Thermoregulatory Centre

Core body temperature too low

Blood vessels in skin dilate (become wider) increasing heat loss. Sweat glands release sweat which evaporates causing cooling.

Blood vessels in skin constrict (become narrower) reducing heat loss. Muscles start to 'shiver' causing heat energy to be released via respiration in cells.

In Hot Conditions

Greater blood flow through superficial capillaries

Sweat

Sweat gland

Shunt vessel closed

In Cold Conditions

Reduced blood flow through superficial capillaries

Sweating stopped

Sweat gland

Shunt vessel open

The shunt vessel acts as a bypass valve to regulate the flow of blood through the superficial capillaries

You need to be able to evaluate the data from the experiments by Banting and Best which led to the discovery of insulin.

In the early 20th century, it was discovered that the pancreas played a part in diabetes.

Shortly after this discovery, Frederick Banting and Charles Best worked in the University of Toronto (in Canada) conducting experiments on dogs to discover what would happen when they removed their pancreases. As they expected, the dogs developed diabetes.

Banting and Best then developed treatments to test on the dogs. They extracted many compounds from the islets of Langerhans (cells in the pancreas which produce insulin). These compounds were then injected into the diabetic dogs to try to find the hormone that would reverse their diabetes. New methods of testing blood sugar levels allowed them to accurately determine what effects their treatments were having on the dogs.

At the start, the injections were not pure and often the dog died. With the help of a group of researchers, they were eventually able to make an extract that was pure enough to try on a human patient.

In 1922, they announced that they had discovered insulin and a 14-year old boy was successfully treated for diabetes in Toronto Hospital with the extract that they called insulin.

Even without the data from their experiments, it is possible to evaluate how accurate and reliable the data they obtained would have been by looking at the methods they used.

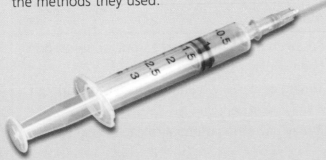

Advantages of their Methods

- They repeated their experiments and obtained the same results, which shows that the evidence is reliable.
- They carried out all their experiments on the same animal species.

Disadvantages of their Methods

- All their experiments were carried out on dogs; there was no guarantee that the same results would be produced in humans.
- Initially, they could not control the purity of the extract they produced.
- The equipment they were using to measure blood sugar is unlikely to be as accurate as modern technology.
- They had only treated one person successfully with the insulin when they announced they had found a treatment – it could have been due to other factors.

How Science Works

You need to be able to evaluate modern methods of treating diabetes.

Example

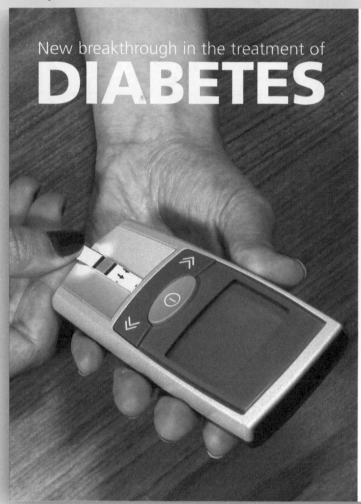

New breakthrough in the treatment of

DIABETES

Diabetes affects about 2 million people in the UK, including up to 1 million who are unaware that they are diabetic.

There are two types of diabetes. Type 1 diabetes develops suddenly, usually at a young age. People with Type 1 diabetes need daily injections of insulin throughout their lives since their bodies do not produce enough insulin. They also require a healthy diet with the right balance of foods. Type 2 diabetes develops gradually and tends to affect people over 40 who are often overweight or obese. Type 2 diabetes can usually be controlled through diet and exercise alone but, in some cases, people with Type 2 diabetes may also need insulin injections.

Although with practice most people find giving themselves injections pain-free and simple, it can be difficult for those who need up to four insulin injections a day. Further difficulties are often encountered with injecting, as the absorption of insulin into the bloodstream can be affected by a number of factors. These include the site of the injection (insulin is absorbed quickest from the abdomen), and using the correct injection technique (if it is too shallow into the skin, or too deep into the muscle, the insulin will not be absorbed properly). Smoking can cause inconsistent blood glucose levels as nicotine causes changes in small blood vessels which may affect absorption.

However, a new breakthrough treatment is being developed, which would allow powdered insulin to be taken through an inhaler. This could be a fantastic step forward for all insulin users, and would reduce problems associated with injections.

Research carried out on inhaled insulin found that the doses produced regular concentrations of insulin. However, there are problems too, for example, the timing of doses would be difficult to assess as the response to a dose may not be easy to predict. Inhaling insulin may prove to be expensive, due to the large doses required, whilst another concern is that it may have the potential to cause lung cancer.

Injected Insulin

Benefits

- Treatment has been used successfully for many years.
- Most people find injecting themselves painless and fairly easy.

Problems

- People must learn the correct way to inject, which can be difficult.
- Some people need to inject themselves up to four times a day, which can be inconvenient.
- Absorption into the bloodstream can be affected by the site of the injection.
- Further problems can be encountered if the person smokes.

Inhaled Insulin

Benefits

- People don't have to inject themselves.
- May lead to the development of other methods of administering insulin.
- In tests, the inhaled doses produced consistent concentrations of insulin.

Problems

- Research is still being carried out, so it has not been widely used yet.
- Timing of doses would be difficult to work out.
- It may be expensive.
- It may have the potential to cause lung cancer.

11.8

Which human characteristics show a simple pattern of inheritance?

Certain genetic disorders and the sex of a baby show a simple pattern of inheritance. To understand this, you need to know…

- the difference between body cells and sex cells in terms of chromosomes
- what meiosis and mitosis are
- why sexual reproduction promotes variation
- how genes control sex and characteristics
- what alleles, chromosomes and DNA are
- how certain disorders are inherited, and how embryo screening can identify these disorders.

Body cells contain **46 chromosomes** arranged as **23 pairs**. Chromosomes are made up of large molecules of **DNA**. A **gene** is a section of DNA.

Gametes – female eggs and male sperm – have 23 chromosomes (one from each pair). The fusion of these two cells produces a **zygote** with 46 chromosomes in total (23 pairs).

Inheritance of Sex – the Sex Chromosome

Of the 23 pairs of chromosomes in human body cells, one pair is the sex chromosomes.

- In females, these are identical and are called the X chromosomes.
- In males, one is much shorter than the other. The shorter one is called the Y chromosome and the longer one is called the X chromosome.

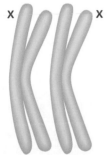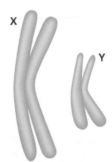

Female Sex Chromosomes   **Male Sex Chromosomes**

Pairs of Chromosomes in a Male

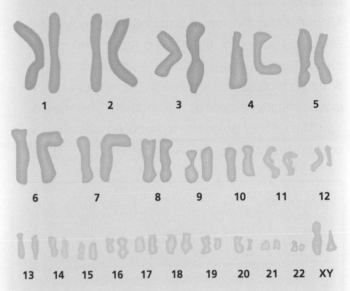

Like all pairs of chromosomes, offspring inherit one sex chromosome from the mother and one from the father.

Ultimately, therefore, the sex of an individual is decided by whether the ovum is fertilised by an X-carrying sperm or a Y-carrying sperm.

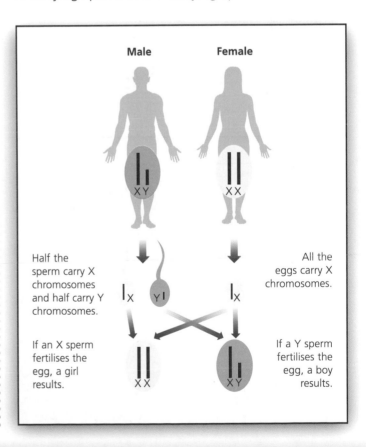

Male   Female

Half the sperm carry X chromosomes and half carry Y chromosomes.

All the eggs carry X chromosomes.

If an X sperm fertilises the egg, a girl results.

If a Y sperm fertilises the egg, a boy results.

Biology Unit 2

Cell Division

Mitosis

Mitosis is the division of body cells to produce new cells. This occurs for growth and repair (and also in asexual reproduction). Before the cell divides, a copy of each chromosome is made so the new cell has exactly the same genetic information. This means that the cells of asexually reproduced offspring contain the same genes as the parents.

Fertilisation

When gametes join at fertilisation, one chromosome comes from each parent and a single body cell with new pairs of chromosomes is formed.

This then divides repeatedly by mitosis to form a new individual, giving rise to variation.

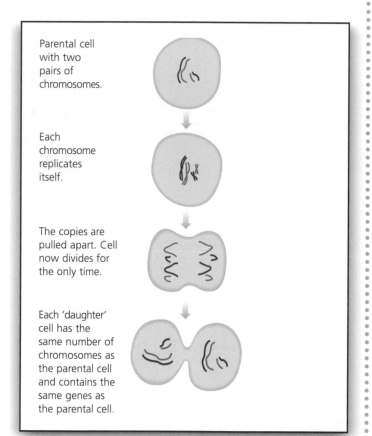

Parental cell with two pairs of chromosomes.

Each chromosome replicates itself.

The copies are pulled apart. Cell now divides for the only time.

Each 'daughter' cell has the same number of chromosomes as the parental cell and contains the same genes as the parental cell.

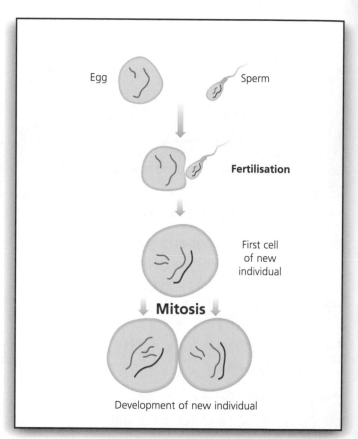

Egg   Sperm

Fertilisation

First cell of new individual

Mitosis

Development of new individual

Meiosis

This occurs in the testes and ovaries. The cells in these organs divide to produce the gametes (eggs and sperm) for sexual reproduction.

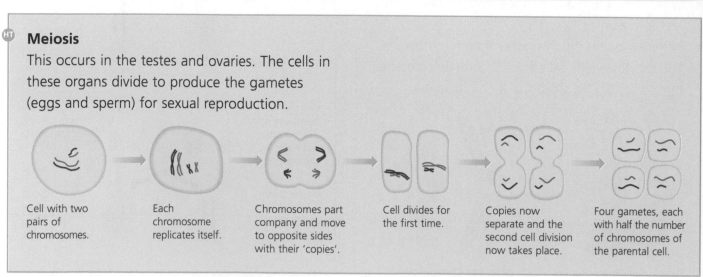

Cell with two pairs of chromosomes.

Each chromosome replicates itself.

Chromosomes part company and move to opposite sides with their 'copies'.

Cell divides for the first time.

Copies now separate and the second cell division now takes place.

Four gametes, each with half the number of chromosomes of the parental cell.

Genetics

Alleles

Some genes have different forms or variations – these are called **alleles**. For example, the gene that controls whether you can roll your tongue or not has two alleles (or forms) – you either can or you can't. Similarly, in the gene for eye colour there are two alleles – blue or brown.

In a pair of chromosomes, the alleles for a gene can be the same or different. If they are different, then one allele will be **dominant** and one allele will be **recessive**. The dominant allele will control the characteristics of the gene. A recessive allele will only control the characteristics of the gene if it is present on both chromosomes in a pair (i.e. no dominant allele is present).

Example: Dominant and Recessive Alleles

Here are three pairs of genes from the middle of a pair of chromosomes. These are the genes which code for tongue-rolling ability, eye colour, and type of earlobe.

- **Dominant alleles** express themselves even if present only once so an individual can be **homozygous dominant** (BB) or **heterozygous** (Bb) for brown eyes.
- **Recessive alleles** express themselves only if present twice so an individual can only be **homozygous recessive** (bb) for blue eyes.

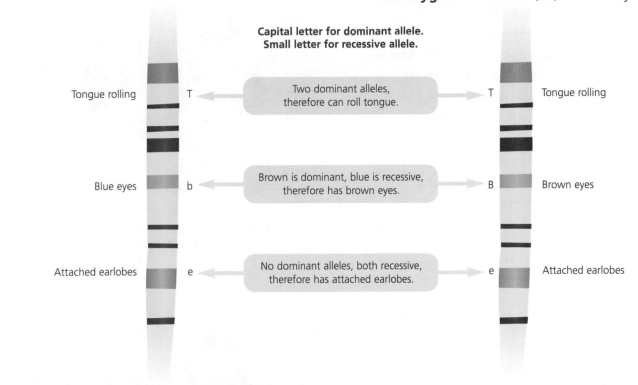

**Capital letter for dominant allele.
Small letter for recessive allele.**

Tongue rolling — T — Two dominant alleles, therefore can roll tongue. — T — Tongue rolling

Blue eyes — b — Brown is dominant, blue is recessive, therefore has brown eyes. — B — Brown eyes

Attached earlobes — e — No dominant alleles, both recessive, therefore has attached earlobes. — e — Attached earlobes

This table shows the possible combinations:

	Homozygous dominant	**Heterozygous**	**Homozygous recessive**
Tongue rolling	TT (can roll)	Tt (can roll)	tt (can't roll)
Eye colour	BB (brown)	Bb (brown)	bb (blue)
Ear lobes	EE (free lobes)	Ee (free lobes)	ee (attached lobes)

Biology Unit 2

Monohybrid Inheritance

As we saw on previous pages, genes exist in pairs; one on each chromosome in a pair. We call these pairs of genes 'alleles' when they code for alternatives of the same characteristic, e.g. eye colour. When a characteristic is determined by just one pair of alleles then simple genetic crosses can be performed to investigate the mechanism of inheritance. This type of inheritance is referred to as **monohybrid inheritance**.

Inheritance of Eye Colour

In genetic diagrams we use capital letters for dominant alleles and lower case for recessive alleles. In eye colour, therefore, we use 'B' for brown eye alleles and 'b' for blue eye alleles.

From the crosses on the diagrams opposite it can be seen that...

- if one parent has two dominant genes then all the offspring will inherit that characteristic
- if both parents have one recessive gene then this characteristic may appear in the offspring (a one in four chance)
- if one parent has a recessive gene and the other has two recessive genes, then there is a 50% chance of that characteristic appearing.

But remember, these are only probabilities. In practice, all that matters is which egg is fertilised by which sperm, and that is completely random.

> **HT** These are the typical examples you may be asked about in your exam. When you construct genetic diagrams remember to...
> - clearly identify the alleles of the parents
> - place each of these alleles in a separate gamete
> - join each gamete with the two gametes from the other parent.

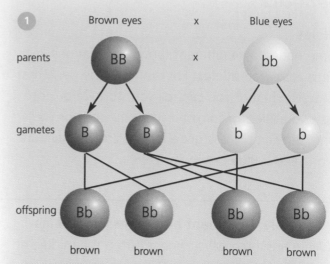

1. 100% chance of offspring having brown eyes.

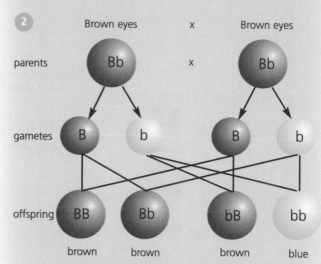

2. 75% chance of offspring having brown eyes, 25% chance of offspring having blue eyes.

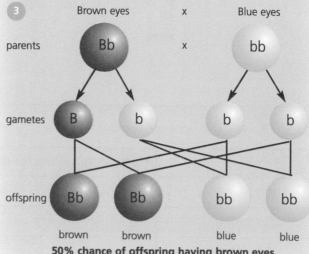

3. 50% chance of offspring having brown eyes, 50% chance of offspring having blue eyes.

Differentiation of Cells

When cells develop a specialised structure to carry out a specific function, this is **differentiation**.

- Most plant cells can differentiate throughout life.
- Animal cells differentiate at an early stage so quickly become muscle, nerves, etc.

Mature cells usually divide for repair and replacement.

Stem Cells

Stem cells are cells in human embryos and adult bone marrow, which have yet to differentiate. They can be made to differentiate into many different types of cells, e.g. a nerve cell, so treatment with these cells may help conditions such as paralysis.

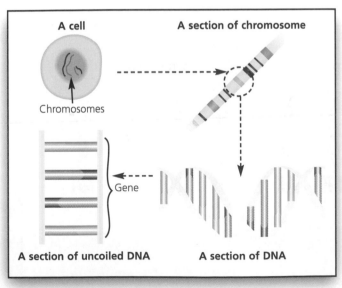

Stem cell / Nerve cell / Muscle cell / Skin cell

Genes, Chromosomes and DNA

In normal human cells, there are only 23 pairs of chromosomes. They consist of long, coiled molecules of **DNA** (Deoxyribonucleic acid).

The DNA molecule itself consists of two strands which are coiled to form a **double helix**.

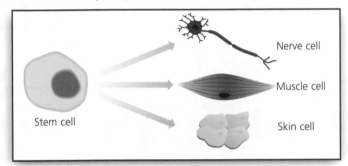

A cell / Chromosomes / **A section of chromosome** / Gene / **A section of uncoiled DNA** / **A section of DNA**

Genes are sections of DNA which code for a particular inherited characteristic, e.g. blue eyes.

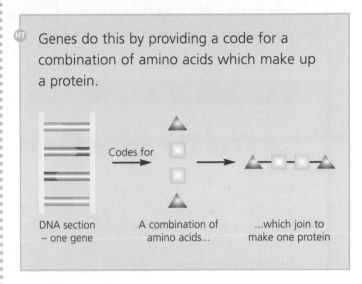

HT Genes do this by providing a code for a combination of amino acids which make up a protein.

Codes for

DNA section – one gene / A combination of amino acids... / ...which join to make one protein

Each person has unique DNA (apart from identical twins which have the same DNA), which means it can be used for DNA fingerprinting (identification).

Genetic Disorders

Embryos can be screened for the genes that cause genetic disorders.

- **Huntington's Disease**
  Huntington's disease is a disorder of the nervous system caused by a dominant allele. It can be passed on by only one parent who has the disorder.
- **Cystic Fibrosis**
  Cystic fibrosis is a disorder of cell membranes. It must be inherited from both parents, who can be carriers without having the disorder themselves. It is caused by a recessive allele.

A person with cystic fibrosis using an inhaler

You need to be able to explain why Mendel proposed the idea of separately inherited factors and why the importance of this discovery was not recognised until after his death.

ScienceMonthly Edition 2

Understanding Genetics

The start of modern genetics was marked by Gregor Mendel's research on pea plants in 1865. He investigated the height of pea plants which were all either tall or dwarf.

He began by taking a plant which was pure-breeding for tallness (i.e. when bred with itself or other tall plants they only produced tall plants) and a plant which was pure-breeding for dwarfness (see diagram 1 below).

He cross-fertilised these plants by taking pollen from each one. To his surprise, all the plants produced from the cross-fertilisation were tall (see diagram 2 below), which led to Mendel's first law:

'When pure-breeding plants with contrasting traits are cross-fertilised, all the offspring will resemble one of the parents.'

Mendel then crossed several of the tall plants that he had produced. Again, he was surprised to find that there were three tall plants to every dwarf plant (see diagram 3 below). He based his second law on this, stating:

'For every trait, every individual must have two determiners.'

Mendel's work was not recognised in his lifetime because much of his research was carried out in his spare time. He worked alone with no one to assist him and when he sent the results of his research to a renowned German botanist he was advised that he needed more data. His results came from over 21000 plants!

His work was discovered in 1900, 16 years after his death, by a team of scientists looking for evidence to support Charles Darwin's *'Origin of the Species'*. They considered Mendel's work to be of great importance because...

- he had planned his experiments on a large scale to eliminate chance effects
- his choice of plants was ideal since the peas showed definite characteristics and were not susceptible to disease and weather factors
- he used only pure-breeding plants to start his work.

The 'determiners' that Mendel had written about are what are now known as genes. The

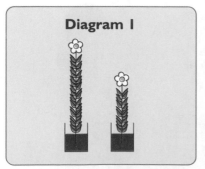

Diagram 1

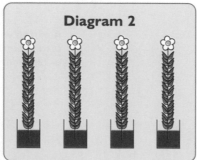

Diagram 2

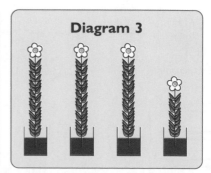

Diagram 3

You need to be able to make informed judgements about the social and ethical issues concerning the use of stem cells from embryos in medical research and treatments.

Most adult cells in the body have a specific function and structure which cannot be changed, for example, muscle cells cannot become nerve cells.

Stem cells are different. They are still at an early stage of development, which means they have not yet developed a special structure and function. Scientists are currently carrying out research which should eventually make it possible to use stem cells to generate healthy tissue to replace tissue that has been damaged, either by trauma or disease. Some of the conditions which scientists believe may eventually be treated by stem cell therapy are Parkinson's disease, Alzheimer's disease, heart disease, stroke, arthritis, diabetes, burns and spinal cord damage.

There is great debate about the use of stem cells; you have to form your own opinion based on evidence and understand that science can help us in many ways but it cannot supply all the answers.

To help you to make an informed decision, the table below contains some reasons for and against the use of stem cells.

A magnified stem cell.

For	Against
• The embryos from which the stem cells are taken are grown in laboratories and are only a few days old; many people see them simply as microscopic balls of cells. • Embryos provide the most useful stem cells: the cells are non-specialised, which means they can become any specific type of cell (adult stem cells are more limited in their potential uses). • They can act as a repair kit for damaged tissue. • Stem cells may be able to treat many diseases and conditions in the future.	• Many people believe it is morally wrong to experiment on embryos (even those grown in the laboratory) as they could all potentially develop into a baby. • Stem cells are cultivated using nutrients from animal sources, which could carry diseases that could be passed to humans. • People who receive cell transplants through stem cell therapy could be infected with viruses. • Stem cells may turn cancerous.

You need to be able to make informed judgements about the economic, social and ethical issues concerning embryo screening.

Embryo Screening

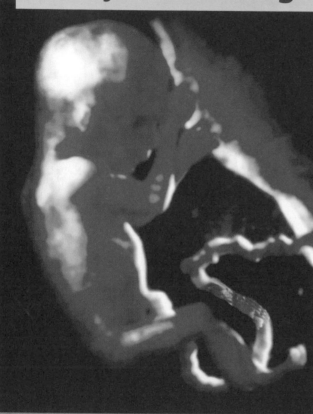

Embryos can be screened during the course of pregnancy. Screening can also take place at the eight-cell stage of development of an IVF (in vitro fertilisation) embryo before it is implanted into the mother's womb. This type of screening is called Pre-implantation Genetic Diagnosis (PGD). This type of screening is currently permitted in order to detect inherited diseases such as Huntington's disease and cystic fibrosis.

The Human Fertilisation and Embryology Authority is now asking if embryos should also be checked for genes linked to cancer and the early onset of Alzheimer's disease. Carrying these genes does not mean a person will definitely develop disease, but it puts them at an increased risk.

A mother who lost an eye as a child because she had retinoblastoma (eye cancer) passed on the gene to her first son, who underwent chemotherapy to get rid of the cancer. Now fertility experts at a London hospital have been given authorisation to test her embryos to find out if any of her future children are at risk of contracting the disease.

There is a fear that this type of screening could be used to detect other genetic factors, which could lead to a 'designer baby' culture, where babies who do not have the desired attributes could be aborted.

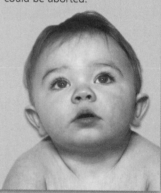

When making judgements on embryo screening, you should consider social, ethical and economic issues. Some are listed in the table below.

Advantages	Disadvantages
• Doctors can determine whether a child will have an increased risk of contracting a particular illness or disease. • It prepares parents for the possibility of a child developing a disorder, disease or illness. • Carriers of genetic disorders could make informed decisions about whether to have children.	• Could result in unborn children being aborted if their genetic make-up is 'faulty'. • Parents may want to choose the genetic make-up of their child. • It has the potential to be used to determine who can / cannot reproduce. • It could stigmatise and upset people to learn they carry a genetic disorder, disease or illness.

HT **You need to be able to predict / explain the outcome of crosses between individuals for each possible combination of dominant and recessive alleles of the same gene, and construct genetic diagrams.**

Example

If a gene for retinoblastoma (a type of cancer affecting the eye) is present in an individual, there is a 90% chance that they will develop the disease.

To find out the likelihood of a child receiving this gene, we can construct a simple genetic diagram.

When constructing genetic diagrams, it is important to use the upper case and lower case of the same letter, so you can easily see which is the dominant gene. The gene that causes retinoblastoma is dominant so we will call this 'R' and the normal gene which does not cause the disease, 'r'. These are alleles since they control the same characteristic and are found in pairs. The possible combinations for these alleles are...

RR – child has the retinoblastoma gene
Rr – child has the retinoblastoma gene
rr – child does not have the retinoblastoma gene.

In this example, the father does not have the disease so his gene pair must be rr. The mother has the disease so her gene pair must be RR or Rr.

To calculate the chance of an embryo carrying the gene for retinoblastoma we need to draw two genetic diagrams to show all the possibilities (see opposite).

Remember, even if an individual does have the gene for retinoblastoma, there is still a 10% chance that they will not develop the disease. And experts say nine out of ten cases of the disease can be cured. This raises questions about the ethics of using technology to genetically screen embryos (see p.38).

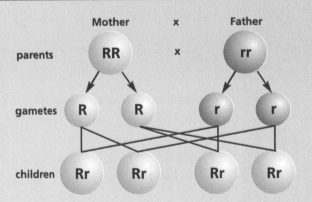

All of the crosses have an 'R' gene, so there is a 100% chance that a child will have the retinoblastoma gene.

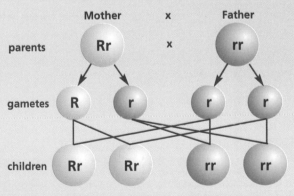

Half of the crosses produce 'Rr' and half produce 'rr', which means that there is a 50% chance that a child will have the retinoblastoma gene.

Example Questions

For Biology Unit 2, you will have to complete one written paper with structured questions.

1 An investigation was carried out to see what effect varying the water content in the soil would have on the height of five tomato plants.

The following results were obtained.

Water content of soil	Height of tomato plants (cm)
Dry	40
Damp	55
Fairly wet	75
Very wet	75
Flooded	60

(a) What was the independent variable in the test?

The water content in the soil.

(1 mark)

(b) What was the dependent variable in the test?

The height of the tomato plants.

(1 mark)

(c) What conclusion can you draw from the investigation?

Fairly wet or very wet soil produces the tallest tomato plants.

(1 mark)

(d) Identify one problem with the method of the investigation.

Only one tomato plant was used in each condition OR There was no accurate measure of the water content in the soil, so the investigation could not be repeated OR We do not know if the tomato plants were the same height or age at the beginning of the investigation.

(1 mark)

(e) Suggest one way in which you could improve the reliability of the results.

Use more plants in each condition OR Measure the amount of water put into the soil, using a measuring cylinder OR Use plants that are all the same height to start off with OR measure the increase in height for each plant.

(1 mark)

5

1 Read the information carefully to make sure you understand what the data in a table shows before answering any questions.

2 The independent variable is the one that is being controlled.

3 The dependent variable is the one that is measured each time the independent variable is changed.

4 Describe what the data tells you – nothing else!

5 You only need to give **one** answer here, but there are lots of possible problems. Think about what you would need to do to improve the reliability and accuracy of the data.

6 This question relates to part (d). Think about how the problem you mentioned could be minimised or solved.

Aerobic respiration – respiration using oxygen which releases energy and produces CO_2 and water

Allele – an alternative form of a particular gene

Amylase – an enzyme that breaks down starch

Anaerobic respiration – incomplete breakdown of glucose without oxygen to produce a small amount of energy very quickly

Bile – a greenish-yellow fluid produced by the liver

Biomass – the mass of a plant or animal minus the water content

Bone marrow – soft tissue in spongy bone

Capillary – the narrowest type of blood vessel

Catalyst – a substance that increases the rate of a chemical reaction without being changed itself

Cell – a fundamental unit of a living organism

Chlorophyll – the green pigment found in most plants, responsible for photosynthesis

Chloroplast – tiny structures in the cytoplasm of plants cells which contains chlorophyll

Community – the total collection of living organisms within a defined area or habitat

Constrict – to compress; make narrow or tight

Core temperature – the main operating temperature of an organism, in comparison to temperatures of peripheral tissues

Cytoplasm – the substance found in living cells (outside the nucleus) where chemical reactions take place

Decay – to rot or decompose

Detritus – organic material formed from dead and decomposing plants and animals

Differentiate – to make / become different

Diffusion – the moving of particles from high to low concentration

DNA – nucleic acid which contains the genetic information carried by every cell

Environment – the conditions around an organism

Enzyme – a protein catalyst which alters the rate of a particular biochemical reaction

Fertilisation – the fusion of the male gamete with the female gamete

Food chain – the feeding relationship between organisms in an ecosystem

Gamete – a specialised sex cell formed by meiosis

Insoluble – a substance that will not dissolve in a solvent

Limiting factors – the main factors that can affect the rate, e.g. of photosynthesis: light intensity; carbon dioxide concentration; temperature

Lipase – an enzyme which breaks down fat into fatty acids and glycerol

Meiosis – cell division that forms daughter cells with half the chromosome number of the parent cell

Microorganism – very small organisms

Mitochondria – the structure in the cytoplasm where energy is produced from chemical reactions

Mitosis – cell division that forms two daughter cells, each with the same number of chromosomes as the parent cell

Neutralise – to make the pH level neutral (pH7)

Nitrate – any compound containing nitrogen

Nucleus – the control centre of a cell

Organ – a collection of tissues which work together to perform a function in the organism, e.g. heart

Osmosis – the movement of water from a dilute to a more concentrated solution across a selectively permeable membrane

Permeable – allows a substance to pass through

pH – measure of the strength of an acid or alkali

Photosynthesis – the chemical process where water combines with carbon dioxide to produce glucose using light energy

Protease – an enzyme used to break down proteins into amino acids

Ribosomes – small structures found in the cytoplasm of living cells, where protein synthesis takes place

Soluble – a substance that dissolves in water to form a solution

Specialised – developed for a special function

Thermoregulation – maintenance of a constant body temperature in warm-blooded animals

Tissue – a collection of similar cells which perform a specific function, e.g. skin tissue

Urea – toxin produced when proteins are broken down

Urine – waste product produced by kidneys

Vacuole – a fluid-filled sac found in cytoplasm

Chemistry Unit 2

How do subatomic particles help us to understand the structure of substances?

The arrangement of electrons in an atom can be used to explain what happens when elements react. To understand this, you need to know...
- about protons, neutrons and electrons
- about shells / energy levels in atoms
- the difference between a compound and a mixture
- about the structures that compounds can make.

How do structures influence the properties and uses of substances?

Substances can be held together by different structures, which have different properties. The forces between bonds are strong; the forces between molecules are weaker. Nanomaterials are very small materials with new properties. To understand this, you need to know...
- that substances can be solids, liquids or gases
- the structures of compounds
- how substances can conduct electricity
- about the developments in nanoscience.

Subatomic Particles

The diagram below shows the subatomic particles in an atom of helium.

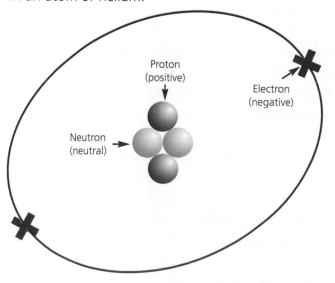

Atoms have a small central nucleus which is made up of protons and neutrons. The nucleus is surrounded by electrons. Protons, neutrons and electrons have relative electrical charges.

Atomic Particle		Relative Charge
Proton		+1
Neutron		0
Electron		-1

All atoms of a particular element contain an equal number of protons and electrons, which means that atoms have no overall charge.

All atoms of a particular element have the same number of protons. Atoms of different elements have different numbers of protons. This is known as their **atomic number**. Elements are arranged in the modern periodic table in order of the number of their atoms.

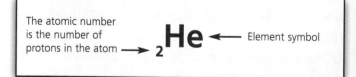

The atomic number is the number of protons in the atom → $_2$He ← Element symbol

Electron configuration tells us how the electrons are arranged around the nucleus in energy levels or shells.

The electrons in an atom occupy the lowest available energy levels (i.e. the innermost available shells).

- The first level or shell can only contain a maximum of 2 electrons.
- The energy levels or shells after this can hold a maximum of 8 electrons.

We write the electron configuration as a series of numbers, e.g. oxygen is 2, 6 and aluminium is 2, 8, 3.

Electronic Structure

The periodic table arranges the elements in terms of their electronic structure. Elements in the same group have the same number of electrons in their outermost shell (this number also coincides with the group number). Elements in the same group therefore have similar properties. From left to right, across each period, a particular energy level is gradually filled with electrons. In the next period, the next energy level is filled etc.

The Alkali Metals (Group 1)

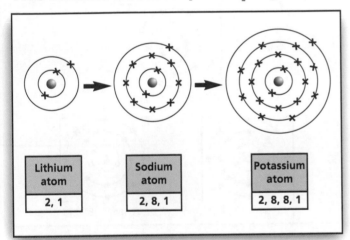

Lithium atom	Sodium atom	Potassium atom
2, 1	2, 8, 1	2, 8, 8, 1

They all have similar properties, because they have the same number of electrons (one) in their outermost shell, i.e. the highest occupied energy level contains one electron. They react with non-metal elements to form ionic compounds (see p.44), where the metal ion has a single positive charge.

The Halogens (Group 7)

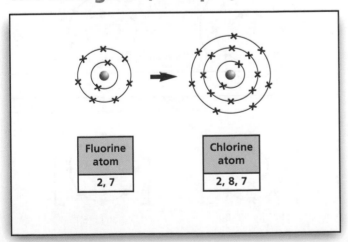

Fluorine atom	Chlorine atom
2, 7	2, 8, 7

They all have similar properties, because they have the same number of electrons (7) in their outermost shell, i.e. the highest occupied energy level contains 7 electrons.

They react with alkali metals to form ionic compounds (see p.44), where the halide ions have a single negative charge.

Mixtures and Compounds

A **mixture** consists of two or more elements or compounds that are not chemically combined. The properties of the substances remain unchanged and specific to that substance.

Compounds are substances in which the atoms of two or more elements are chemically combined (not just mixed together).

Atoms can form chemical bonds by...
• sharing electrons (covalent bonds)
• gaining or losing electrons (ionic bonds).

Either way, when atoms form chemical bonds the arrangement of the outermost shell of electrons changes resulting in each atom getting a complete outer shell of electrons.

For most atoms this is eight electrons but for helium it is only two.

Simple Molecular Compounds

Gases, liquids and solids that have relatively low melting and boiling points consist of simple molecules. Because the molecules have no overall electric charge, they do not conduct electricity.

HT Substances that consist of simple molecules have weak forces of attraction between their molecules (inter-molecular), unlike the very strong bond that exists between two atoms. This is why they have low melting and boiling points.

Chemistry Unit 2

The Ionic Bond

This occurs between a metal and a non-metal atom and involves a **transfer** of electrons from one atom to the other to form electrically charged **ions**, each of which has a complete outermost energy level or shell. This means that ions have the electronic structure of a noble gas. Atoms which **lose electrons** become **positively charged** ions while atoms which **gain electrons** become **negatively charged** ions.

Ionic compounds are giant structures of ions held together by strong forces of attraction between oppositely charged ions that act in all directions. This is called **ionic bonding**. Ionic compounds have high melting and boiling points.

Example 1 – Sodium and chlorine bond ionically to form sodium chloride, NaCl. The sodium (Na) atom has 1 electron in its outer shell which is transferred to the chlorine (Cl) atom so they both have 8 electrons in their outer shell. The atoms become ions Na$^+$ and Cl$^-$ and the compound formed is sodium chloride, NaCl.

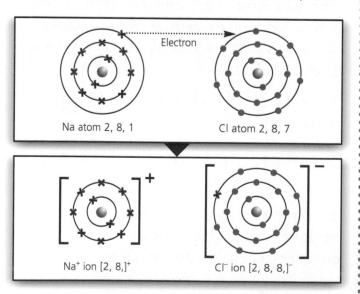

Example 2 – Calcium and chlorine bond ionically to form calcium chloride, CaCl$_2$. The calcium (Ca) atom has 2 electrons in its outer shell and a chlorine (Cl) atom only wants 1 electron therefore 2 Cl atoms are needed to give all 3 atoms 8 electrons in their outer shell. The atoms become ions Ca^{2+}, Cl$^-$ and Cl$^-$ and the compound formed is calcium chloride, CaCl$_2$.

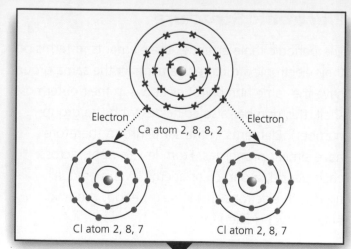

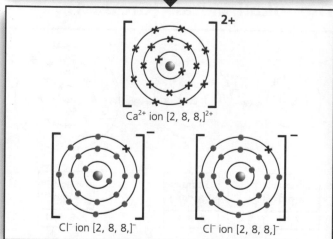

Example 3 – Magnesium and oxygen bond ionically to form magnesium oxide, MgO. The magnesium (Mg) atom has 2 electrons in its outer shell which are transferred to the oxygen (O) atom so they both have 8 electrons in their outer shell. The atoms become ions Mg^{2+} and O^{2-} and the compound formed is magnesium oxide, MgO.

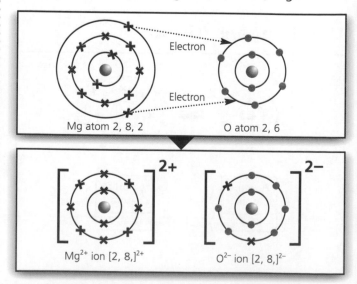

The Covalent Bond

The **covalent bond** is a very strong bond which is formed when electrons are **shared**. This occurs between non-metal atoms.

Some covalently bonded substances have simple bonds (like H_2, Cl_2, O_2, HCl, H_2O, CH_4) whereas others have giant covalent structures, called macromolecules (e.g. diamond, silicon dioxide).

A chlorine atom has 7 electrons in its outermost shell. In order to bond with itself, an electron from each atom is shared to give both chlorine atoms 8 electrons in their outermost shell. This means each atom has a complete outer shell.

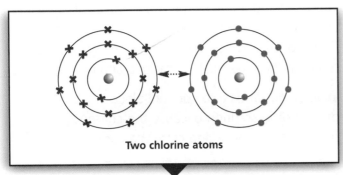

Two chlorine atoms

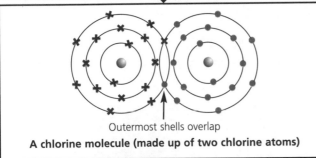

Outermost shells overlap

A chlorine molecule (made up of two chlorine atoms)

Atoms which share electrons often form molecules in which there are strong covalent bonds between the atoms in each molecule but not between molecules. This means that they usually have low melting and boiling points.

Chlorine molecules

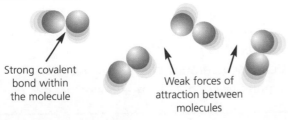

Strong covalent bond within the molecule

Weak forces of attraction between molecules

Covalent Bonding

You need to be familiar with the following examples, and know how to use three different methods for representing the covalent bonds in each molecule. Two forms are given in the examples below:

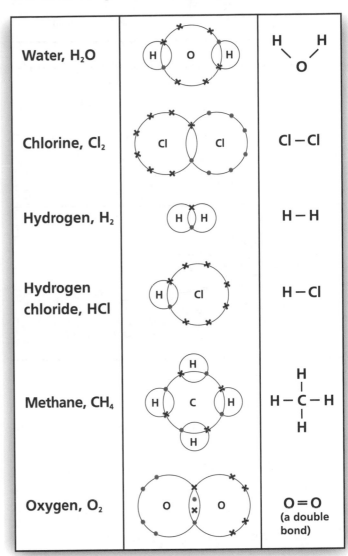

Water, H_2O		H H O
Chlorine, Cl_2		Cl – Cl
Hydrogen, H_2		H – H
Hydrogen chloride, HCl		H – Cl
Methane, CH_4		H H – C – H H
Oxygen, O_2		O = O (a double bond)

The third form of representing covalent bonds is shown here for an ammonia molecule. This is perhaps the most confusing method, and unless specifically asked for, you should use the other two methods.

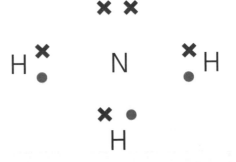

Chemistry Unit 2

Giant Covalent Structures

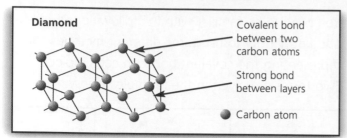

Diamond

Covalent bond between two carbon atoms

Strong bond between layers

● Carbon atom

Diamond is a form of carbon that has a giant, rigid covalent structure (lattice) where each carbon atom forms four covalent bonds with other carbon atoms.

The large number of covalent bonds results in diamond having a very high melting point which makes the diamond very hard.

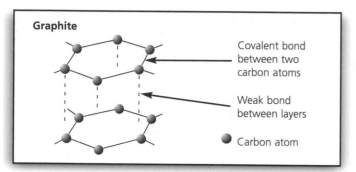

Graphite

Covalent bond between two carbon atoms

Weak bond between layers

● Carbon atom

Graphite is a form of carbon that has a giant covalent structure (lattice) in which each carbon atom forms three covalent bonds with other carbon atoms in a layered structure. The layers can slide past each other, making it soft and slippery.

HT Covalent bonds are very strong. There are weak forces of attraction between layers so one electron from each carbon atom can be delocalised, which allows graphite to conduct heat and electricity.

Silicon Dioxide

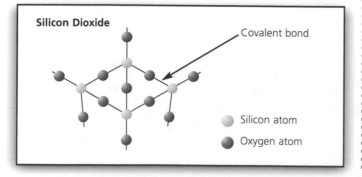

Covalent bond

○ Silicon atom

● Oxygen atom

Silicon dioxide (SiO_2, also known as silica) has a giant, rigid covalent structure (lattice) similar to diamond, where each oxygen atom is joined to two silicon atoms and each silicon atom is joined to four oxygen atoms.

The large number of covalent bonds results in silicon dioxide having a very high melting point.

Giant Ionic Structures

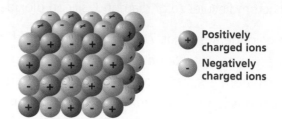

+ **Positively charged ions**
- **Negatively charged ions**

A giant ionic structure is a regular structure (giant ionic lattice) held together by the strong forces of attraction (electrostatic forces) between oppositely charged ions. These forces act in all directions in the lattice. This results in them having high melting and boiling points.

Ionic compounds also conduct electricity when molten or in solution because the charged ions are free to move about and carry the current.

HT ## Metals

Metals have a giant structure in which electrons in the highest energy level can be delocalised.

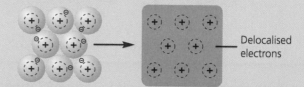

Delocalised electrons

This effectively produces a regular arrangement (lattice) of positive ions that are held together by electrons using electrostatic attraction.

These delocalised electrons…
- hold the atoms together in a regular structure
- allow the atoms to slide over each other so metals can be bent and shaped
- can move around freely, which allows the metal to conduct heat and electricity.

Nanoparticles and Nanostructures

Nanoscience is the study of structures that are 1–100 nanometres in size, roughly in the order of a few hundred atoms. One nanometre is 0.000 000 001m (one billionth of a metre) and is written as 1nm or $1m \times 10^{-9}$. (A human hair is around 20 000nm in diameter and a microbe is around 200nm in diameter.)

Nanoparticles are tiny, tiny particles that can combine to form structures called **nanostructures**.

Nanostructures have always existed in naturally occurring substances such as liposomes, however, they could not be seen until the early 1980s. Scientists working with new technology (the scanning tunnelling microscope) were able to construct enlarged images of surfaces, allowing them to see atoms and molecules for the first time. By the early 1990s, atoms could be isolated and moved. This means nanostructures can be manipulated so materials can be developed that have new and specific properties, and can be used in industry.

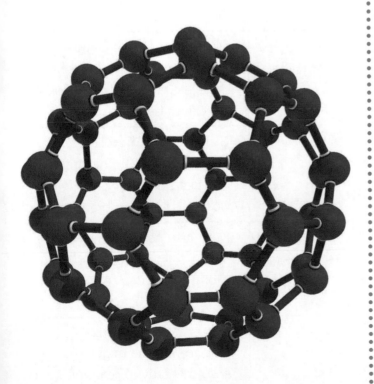

Fullerene related carbon nanostructure

The properties of nanoparticles are different to the properties of the same materials in bulk. For example…

- electrons can move through an insulating layer of atoms
- nanoparticles are more sensitive to light, heat and magnetism
- nanoparticles possess a high surface area in relation to their volume.

A magnified representation of iron atoms in a ring around some surface state electrons

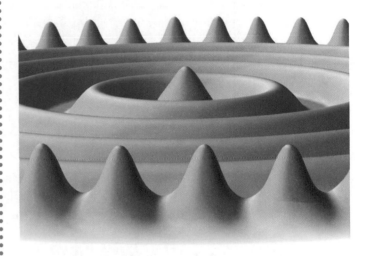

Nanocomposites

Other materials can be added to plastics to make stronger, stiffer and lighter materials, called **nanocomposite** materials. The characteristics of nanocomposites can be seen by looking at the nanostructures formed by the nanoparticles.

Nanocomposites are already being used in the car industry and others are being developed with medical and dental applications in mind. They are also used in energy storage and separation processing, highly selective sensors, new coatings, sunscreens, drug delivery systems, stronger and lighter construction materials, textile fibres and product-specific catalysts.

Smart materials are a type of nanostructure that can be designed so they have specific properties on a nanoscopic scale or behave in a certain way when subjected to certain conditions.

How Science Works

You need to be able to relate the properties of substances to their uses. Suggest the type of structure of a substance when you are given its properties.

*Higher Tier only

Substance	Properties	Example – uses	Structure
Metal	• Strong. • Shiny. • Malleable (bendy). • Good conductor of heat and electricity.*	• Steel – construction. • Gold – jewellery. • Aluminium, copper – pans copper, aluminium – wires. • Copper – pipes, wires.	• The layers of atoms can slide over each other • Metallic bonds between atoms allow delocalised electrons to move freely.*
Non-metal	• Brittle. • Insulator.	• Glass – bottles. • Wood – pan handles.	• Covalent bonds, no ions involved.
Polymer	• Lightweight. • Flexible. • Waterproof.	• Polyethene – plastic bags. • Shaped containers. • Polyvinyl chloride – rainwear.	• Long chain structure of covalent bonded atoms. Forces between them are weak.
Ionic compound	• Hard, crystalline, soluble in water. • High melting points. • Insulator when solid but conducts electricity when molten or dissolved.	• Sodium chloride – food additive. • Sodium chloride – electrolysis.	• Force of attraction between oppositely charged ions formed by electronic transfer. A lattice results which is difficult to break down. In the solid state the ions are held in place. Once melted or dissolved they are free to move.
Molecular covalent	• Soft. • Low melting points. • Insulator.	• Gases. • Ammonia, nitrogen and oxygen gas.	• Molecules with no charge. • Strong bonding inside each molecule but bonding between molecules is weak.
Macromolecules	• Hard. • High melting points.	• Diamond – drill heads. • Silicon dioxide.	• Giant covalent bond. • Huge lattices with millions of covalent bonds. • No weak forces to break.
Nanomaterial	• Very strong. • Huge surface area. • Conduct electricity.	• Nanoparticles – catalysts. • Nanotubes – reinforce tennis rackets, used in computer chips.	• Really tiny particles shaped like hollow balls or closed tubes. • Atoms form covalent bonds leaving free electrons.
Smart material	• Shape memory.	• Nitinol – spectacle frames.	• Can exist in two different solid forms. The molecules absorb energy to rearrange the atoms into a new form.

How Science Works

You need to be able to evaluate developments and applications of new materials, e.g. nanomaterials, smart materials.

New materials are being developed to provide us with materials that have advantageous properties and can therefore be very useful.

The development of nanomaterials is part of nanotechnology (the understanding and control of very small matter). Nanomaterials have many properties which means they have many uses in industry, for example, as industrial catalysts; their very, very small size means they have a large surface area in relation to their size.

Individual nanoparticles have different properties from the whole chemical. They can…

- fill plastics and coat surfaces
- absorb and reflect harmful ultraviolet rays in suncreams and cosmetics
- be added to glass to repel water to keep windows cleaner for longer
- be released in washing machines to clean clothes thoroughly
- be released in fridges to kill micro-organisms and keep food fresher for longer
- be used in sensors, e.g. to test water purity.

Nanotubes which join nanoparticles are very strong. They conduct electricity so they can be used in electric circuits. However, it is important to remember that nanoparticles can be dangerous in certain circumstances, e.g. nanoparticles in water could be dangerous if they are drunk.

Nanotechnology has a wide variety of potential applications in biomedical, optical, and electronic fields. For example, nanotechnology could be used to create secure communication systems, detect and eradicate small tumours, help in the diagnosis of diseases, and in the development of microscopic surgery which would not leave scars.

Nanomaterials can be developed so they have useful properties such as being able to change shape or size as a result of being heated, or changing from a liquid to a solid when near a magnet. These are called smart materials and they can be categorised into different groups – electroactive, thermo-active, and magneto-active – depending on what trigger they respond to. Each type has a different property that can be altered and therefore they each have a different application.

Smart materials can be used in…

- sportswear because they are good thermal insulators as well as being lightweight, breathable and waterproof
- machine designs because they are very reliable, easy to control and fast acting.

New material	Advantages	Disadvantages
Smart Materials (A type of nanomaterial)	• Many different properties. • Many applications. • Easy to manipulate. • Many potential uses to investigate.	• Cost of developing new materials.
Nanomaterials	• Many applications. • Can reduce costs, e.g. when used as catalysts. • Have the potential for many more beneficial uses, especially in the medical industry.	• Difficult to engineer nanoparticles. • Can be dangerous in certain situations, e.g. if get into drinking water. • Could be a danger that nanotechnology could be used to develop materials which could be a cause for concern.

Chemistry Unit 2

12.3

How much can we make and how much do we need?

Atomic mass can be used to calculate the yield from a chemical reaction because we know that no atoms are lost or gained in a chemical reaction. To understand this, you need to know...

- how to find the mass number of an element
- how to find the relative atomic mass
- how to use the relative atomic mass to find the percentage of an element in a compound
- that some reactions can be reversible
- about the Haber process.

Mass Number and Atomic Number

Atoms of an element can be described very conveniently. For example, take the sodium atom...

The mass number is the total number of protons and neutrons in the atom → ^{23}

The atomic number (proton number) is the number of protons in the atom → $_{11}$ **Na** ← Element symbol

| Number of neutrons | = | Mass number | − | Atomic number |

The **atomic number** gives the number of protons, which is equal to the number of electrons. Because atoms have the same number of protons and electrons, they have no overall charge.

Examples

1 Hydrogen
$^{1}_{1}$**H**
1 proton
1 electron
0 neutrons (1-1)

2 Oxygen
$^{16}_{8}$**O**
8 protons
8 electrons
8 neutrons (16-8)

Although protons and electrons balance each other out because they have opposite charges, they do not have equal mass. Protons and neutrons (which together form the nucleus) each have a **relative mass** of 1, whereas the relative mass of an electron is almost nothing.

Atomic Particle		Relative Mass
Proton	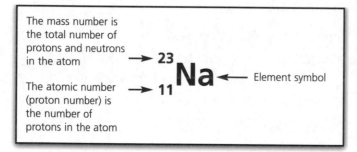	1
Neutron		1
Electron		Very small (negligible)

Isotopes

All atoms of a particular element have the same number of protons; atoms of different elements have different numbers of protons.

However, some atoms of the same element can have different numbers of neutrons. These are called **isotopes**. They are easy to spot because they have the same atomic number but a different mass number.

Examples

1 Chlorine
$^{35}_{17}$**Cl**
17 protons
17 electrons
18 neutrons (35-17)

$^{37}_{17}$**Cl**
17 protons
17 electrons
20 neutrons (37-17)

2 Carbon
$^{12}_{6}$**C**
6 protons
6 electrons
6 neutrons (12-6)

$^{13}_{6}$**C**
6 protons
6 electrons
7 neutrons (13-6)

$^{14}_{6}$**C**
6 protons
6 electrons
8 neutrons (14-6)

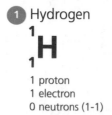

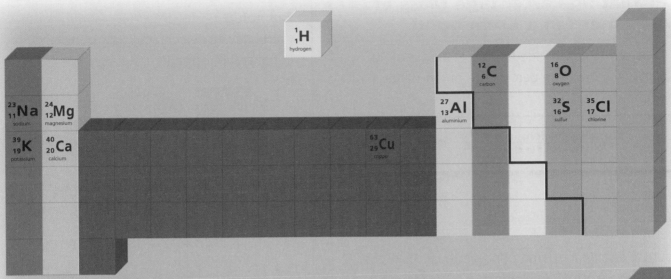

* In some versions of the periodic table this information may be presented slightly differently, e.g.

Relative Atomic Mass, A_r

(HT)

Atoms are too small for their actual atomic mass to be of much use to us. To make things more manageable we use **relative atomic mass, A$_r$**.

Relative atomic mass is the mass of a particular atom compared to a twelfth of the mass of a carbon atom (the ^{12}C isotope). It is an average value for all the isotopes of the element.

The mass number of the element conveniently doubles as the relative atomic mass, A$_r$, of the element. So, if we look at the mass numbers of the chemicals written in the periodic table above, we can see that carbon is 12 times heavier than hydrogen, but is only half as heavy as magnesium, which is three quarters as heavy as sulfur, which is twice as heavy as oxygen, and so on.

We can use relative atomic mass to calculate the relative formula mass (M$_r$) of compounds.

Relative Formula Mass, M_r

The **relative formula mass (M$_r$)** of a compound is simply the relative atomic masses of all its elements added together. To calculate M$_r$, we need the formula of the compound, and the A$_r$ of all the atoms involved.

Example 1

Using the data above, calculate the M$_r$ of water, H_2O.

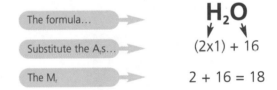

$$H_2O$$
$$(2 \times 1) + 16$$
$$2 + 16 = 18$$

Since water has an M$_r$ of 18, it is 18 times heavier than a hydrogen atom, or one and a half times heavier than a carbon atom, or two thirds as heavy as an aluminium atom.

Example 2

Using the data above, calculate the M$_r$ of potassium carbonate, K_2CO_3.

$$K_2CO_3$$
$$(39 \times 2) + 12 + (16 \times 3)$$
$$78 + 12 + 48 = 138$$

Chemistry Unit 2

Calculating Percentage Mass of an Element in a Compound

If there are 12 left-handed pupils in a class of 30, you can work out the percentage of left-handers in the following way...

$$\frac{\text{Number of left-handers}}{\text{Total number in class}} \times 100\%$$

In this case...

$$\frac{12}{30} \times 100\% = 40\%$$

You use exactly the same principle to calculate the percentage mass of an element in a compound, except this time we express it as...

$$\frac{\text{Relative mass of element in the compound}}{\text{Relative formula mass of compound } (M_r)} \times 100\%$$

The mass of the compound is simply its relative formula mass and all you need to know is the formula of the compound and the relative atomic mass of all the atoms.

Example 1

Calculate the percentage mass of magnesium in magnesium oxide, MgO.

Relative mass of magnesium = 24

Relative formula mass (M_r) of MgO =

$$24 + 16 = 40$$

A_r Mg A_r O A_r MgO

Substituting into our formula...

$$\frac{\text{Relative mass of element}}{M_r \text{ of compound}} \times 100\%$$

$$\frac{24}{40} \times 100\% = 60\%$$

Example 2

Calculate the percentage mass of potassium in potassium carbonate, K_2CO_3.

Relative mass of potassium = 39 x 2

Relative formula mass (M_r) of K_2CO_3 =

$$78 + 12 + 48 = 138$$

A_r K x 2 A_r C A_r O x 3 A_r K_2CO_3

Substituting into our formula...

$$\frac{\text{Relative mass of element}}{M_r \text{ of compound}} \times 100\%$$

$$\frac{78}{138} \times 100\% = 56.5\%$$

Calculating the Empirical Formula of a Compound

The empirical formula of a compound is the simplest formula that represents the composition of the compound by mass.

Example

Find the simplest formula of an oxide of iron produced by reacting 1.12g of iron with 0.48g of oxygen (A_r Fe = 56, A_r O = 16).

Identify the mass of the elements in the compound...

Masses: Fe = 1.12, O = 0.48

Divide these masses by their relative atomic masses...

$$Fe = \frac{1.12}{56} = 0.02 \qquad O = \frac{0.48}{16} = 0.03$$

Identify the ratio of atoms in the compound...

Ratio =   x 100 $0.02 : 0.03$ x 100

$$2 : 3$$

Empirical formula = **Fe_2O_3**

The Mole

A **mole** (**mol**) is a measure of the number of particles (atoms or molecules) contained in a substance. One mole of any substance (element or compound) will always contain the same number of particles – six hundred thousand billion billion or 6×10^{23}. This is the relative formula mass of the substance.

If a substance is an element, the mass of one mole of the substance, called the molar mass (g/mol), is always equal to the relative atomic mass, A_r, of the substance in grams, for example…

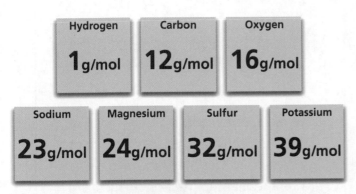

Hydrogen	Carbon	Oxygen
1g/mol	**12**g/mol	**16**g/mol

Sodium	Magnesium	Sulfur	Potassium
23g/mol	**24**g/mol	**32**g/mol	**39**g/mol

If a substance is a compound, the mass of one mole of the substance is always equal to the relative formula mass, M_r (A_rs of all its elements added together), of the substance in grams.

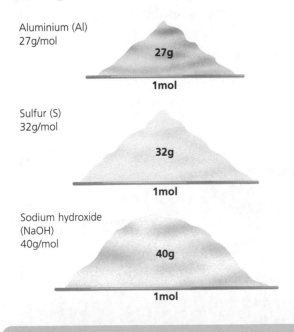

Aluminium (Al)
27g/mol

27g

1mol

Sulfur (S)
32g/mol

32g

1mol

Sodium hydroxide (NaOH)
40g/mol

40g

1mol

A_r sodium + A_r hydrogen + A_r oxygen
= 23 + 1 + 16
= 40

Questions involving moles can be calculated using the following relationship. You need to remember this relationship because it will not be given to you in the examination.

$$\text{Number of moles of substance (mol)} = \frac{\text{Mass of substance (g)}}{\text{Mass of one mole (g/mol)}}$$

Example 1

Calculate the number of moles of carbon in 36g of the element.

Using the relationship…

$$\text{Number of moles of substance (mol)} = \frac{\text{Mass of substance (g)}}{\text{Mass of one mole (g/mol)}}$$

$$= \frac{36g}{12g/mol}$$

A_r carbon = 12

= 3 moles

Example 2

Calculate the number of moles of carbon dioxide in 33g of the gas.

Using the relationship…

$$\text{Number of moles of substance (mol)} = \frac{\text{Mass of substance (g)}}{\text{Mass of one mole (g/mol)}}$$

$$= \frac{33g}{44g/mol}$$

A_r carbon dioxide
= A_r carbon +
2 x A_r oxygen
= 12 + (2 x 16)
= 44

= 0.75 mole

Example 3

Calculate the mass of 4 moles of sodium hydroxide.

Rearranging the relationship…

$$\text{Mass of substance (g)} = \text{Number of moles of substance (mol)} \times \text{Mass of one mole (g/mol)}$$

$$= \text{4mol} \times \text{40g/mol}$$

= 160g

These calculations can also be done using ratios. It depends on how confident you are in your mathematical ability.

Chemistry Unit 2

Calculating the Mass of a Product

Example

Calculate how much calcium oxide can be produced from 50kg of calcium carbonate. (Relative atomic masses: Ca = 40, C = 12, O = 16).

> Write down the equation...

$$CaCO_3 \rightarrow CaO + CO_2$$

> Work out the M_r of each substance...

$$40 + 12 + (3 \times 16) \rightarrow (40 + 16) + [12 + (2 \times 16)]$$

> Check the total mass of reactants equals the total mass of the products. If they are not the same, check your work...

$$100 \rightarrow 56 + 44 ✔$$

> Since the question only mentions calcium oxide and calcium carbonate, you can now ignore the carbon dioxide. You just need the ratio of mass of reactant to mass of product.

$$100 : 56$$

If 100kg of $CaCO_3$ produces 56kg of CaO, then 1kg of $CaCO_3$ produces $\frac{56}{100}$ kg of CaO, and 50kg of $CaCO_3$ produces $\frac{56}{100}$ x 50 = **28kg** of CaO.

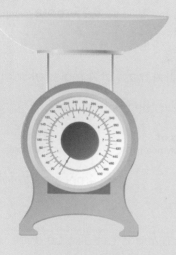

Calculating the Mass of a Reactant

Example

Calculate how much aluminium oxide is needed to produce 540 tonnes of aluminium. (Relative atomic masses: Al = 27, O = 16).

> Write down the equation...

$$2Al_2O_3 \rightarrow 4Al + 3O_2$$

> Work out the M_r of each substance...

$$2[(2 \times 27) + (3 \times 16)] \rightarrow (4 \times 27) + [3 \times (2 \times 16)]$$

> Check the total mass of reactants equals the total mass of the products...

$$204 \rightarrow 108 + 96 ✔$$

> Since the question only mentions aluminium oxide and aluminium, you can now ignore the oxygen. You just need the ratio of mass of reactant to mass of product.

$$204 : 108$$

If 204 tonnes of Al_2O_3 produces 108 tonnes of Al, then $\frac{204}{108}$ tonnes is needed to produce 1 tonne of Al, and $\frac{204}{108}$ x 540 tonnes is needed to produce 540 tonnes of Al, i.e. 1020 tonnes of Al_2O_3 is needed.

Yield

Atoms are never lost or gained in a chemical reaction. However, it is not always possible to obtain the calculated amount of the product because…

- if the reaction is reversible, it may not go to completion
- some product could be lost when it is separated from the reaction mixture
- there could be different ways for the reactants to behave in an expected reaction.

HT The amount of product obtained is called the **yield**. The **percentage yield** can be calculated by comparing the actual yield obtained from a reaction with the maximum theoretical yield.

$$\text{Percentage yield} = \frac{\text{Yield from reaction}}{\text{Maximum theoretical yield}} \times 100$$

Example

We know from the example on p.54 that you would expect to produce 28kg of calcium oxide (CaO) from 50kg of calcium carbonate ($CaCO_3$). This is the maximum theoretical yield.

A company heats 50kg of calcium carbonate in a kiln and obtains 22kg of calcium oxide.

Using the formula, the percentage yield is…

$$\textbf{Percentage yield} = \frac{22}{28} \times 100$$

$$= 78.6\%$$

Calculating Atom Economy

Because chemical reactions often produce more than one product, not all of the starting materials are converted into 'useful' products, e.g. products that can be used in industry.

Atom economy (atom utilisation) is a measure of the amounts of reactants that end up as useful products. This is an important calculation in industry, where the reaction conditions need to give economical and sustainable atom economy.

$$\text{Atom economy} = \frac{M_r \text{ of useful products}}{M_r \text{ of reactants}} \times 100$$

Example

Calcium carbonate → Calcium oxide + Carbon dioxide

In this reaction, calcium oxide is the useful product because it can be used to produce slaked lime (see p.). Calcium dioxide is also produced, but this is a waste product.

To calculate the atom economy of this reaction, first find the relative formula mass (M_r) of all the reactants and products.

$$CaCO_3 \rightarrow CaO + CO_2$$

M_r of $CaCO_3$ = 40 + 12 + (3 x 16) = **100**

M_r of CaO = 40 + 16 = **56**

M_r of CO_2 = 12 + (2 x 16) = **44**

Using the equation…

$$\textbf{Atom economy} = \frac{56}{100} \times 100$$

$$= 56\%$$

44% will be wasted

Chemistry Unit 2

Reversible Reactions

Some chemical reactions are **reversible**, i.e. the products can react to produce the original reactants.

$$A + B \rightleftharpoons C + D$$

A and B react to produce C and D, but also C and D can react to produce A and B. For example...

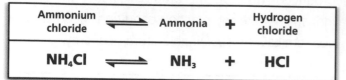

Ammonium chloride	$\rightleftharpoons$	Ammonia	+	Hydrogen chloride
NH_4Cl	$\rightleftharpoons$	NH_3	+	HCl

Solid ammonium chloride decomposes when heated to produce ammonia and hydrogen chloride gas, both of which are colourless (see diagram).

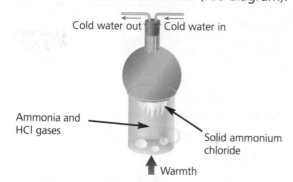

Cold water out   Cold water in

Ammonia and HCl gases

Solid ammonium chloride

Warmth

Ammonia reacts with hydrogen chloride gas to produce clouds of white ammonium chloride powder.

Production of Ammonia – the Haber Process

The raw materials for the Haber Process are...

- nitrogen – from the fractional distillation of liquid air
- hydrogen – from natural gas and steam.

The purified nitrogen and hydrogen are passed over an iron catalyst at a high temperature of about 450°C and a high pressure of about 200 atmospheres. Some of the hydrogen and nitrogen reacts to form ammonia. The ammonia produced can break down again into nitrogen and hydrogen.

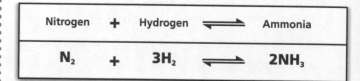

Nitrogen	+	Hydrogen	$\rightleftharpoons$	Ammonia
N_2	+	$3H_2$	$\rightleftharpoons$	$2NH_3$

HT These reaction conditions are chosen to produce a reasonable yield of ammonia quickly, but even so, only some of the hydrogen and nitrogen react together to form ammonia.

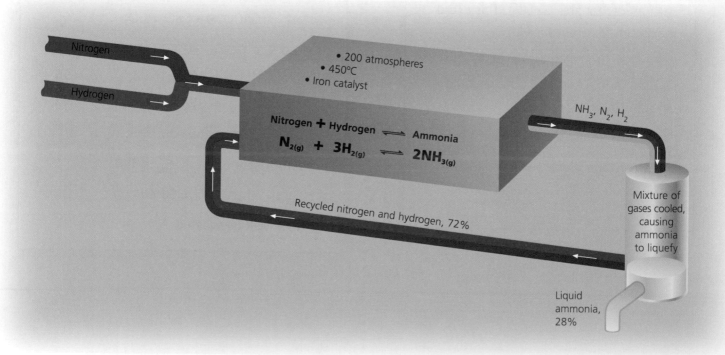

Nitrogen

Hydrogen

- 200 atmospheres
- 450°C
- Iron catalyst

Nitrogen + Hydrogen $\rightleftharpoons$ Ammonia

$$N_{2(g)} + 3H_{2(g)} \rightleftharpoons 2NH_{3(g)}$$

NH_3, N_2, H_2

Mixture of gases cooled, causing ammonia to liquefy

Recycled nitrogen and hydrogen, 72%

Liquid ammonia, 28%

HT **You need to be able to calculate chemical quantities involving formula mass (M_r) and calculate the atom economy for industrial processes and evaluate sustainable development issues relating to this economy.**

Ethyl ethanoate is used as a solvent in glues and nail polish removers. It is produced by the following reaction:

Ethanoic acid	+	Ethanol	→	Ethyl ethanoate	+	Water
$C_2H_4O_2$	+	C_2H_6O	→	$C_4H_8O_2$	+	H_2O

To calculate the atom economy of this reaction we first need to work out the formula masses of the reactants and the useful product (ethyl ethanoate).

M_r of $C_2H_4O_2$ = (2 x 12) + (4 x 1) + (2 x 16) = **60**
M_r of C_2H_6O = (2 x 12) + (6 x 1) + 16 = **46**
M_r of $C_4H_8O_2$ = (4 x 12) + (8 x 1) + (2 x 16) = **88**

Now use the following formula to calculate the atom economy:

$$\text{Atom economy} = \frac{M_r \text{ of useful products}}{M_r \text{ of reactants}} \times 100\%$$

$$\text{Atom economy} = \frac{88}{(60 + 46)} \times 100\% = 83\%$$ **17% will be wasted**

In industry, research scientists measure or calculate the amounts of materials used and produced in reactions to make sure the reactions are economical. If a reaction does not convert all of the reactants into useful products, there will be some wastage. As a result, the manufacturer might have to raise the sell-on price of the product, and this will have an impact on the retail price of all the final products it is used in.

It is important that chemical reactions which are part of industrial processes are as economical as possible, so that the product costs the people who need to buy it, as little as possible.

It is also important to plan for meeting the present needs of people without spoiling the environment. This is called a sustainable development. The Earth only has a finite supply of minerals, so it makes sense to only use as much as we need. Therefore, industries aim to use smaller amounts of raw materials and energy while creating less waste.

Scientists in industry look for ways to use the waste products so that they become useful by-products of the reaction.

The chemical industry examines its processes carefully to make sure that it...
- makes efficient use of energy
- reduces the hazards and risks of the chemicals it uses and makes
- reduces waste
- attempts to convert a high proportion of the atoms in the reactants into the products
- uses mainly renewable resources
- prevents pollution of the environment.

Chemistry Unit 2

12.4

How can we control the rates of chemical reactions?

Controlling the rate of reactions is very important in industry. To understand this, you need to know...

- how to find the rate of a chemical reaction
- what factors affect the rate of reaction
- how catalysts are used to alter the rate of chemical reactions.

Rates of Reactions

Chemical reactions only occur when reacting particles collide with each other with sufficient energy. The minimum amount of energy required to cause a reaction is called the **activation energy**. There are four important factors which affect the rate of reaction:

- temperature
- concentration
- surface area
- use of a catalyst.

Temperature of the Reactants

Low Temperature	High Temperature
In a cold reaction mixture, the particles are moving quite slowly – the particles will collide with each other less often, with less energy, so fewer collisions will be successful.	If we heat the reaction mixture, the particles will move more quickly – the particles will collide with each other more often, with greater energy, so many more collisions will be successful.

Concentration of the Dissolved Reactants

Low Concentration	High Concentration
In a reaction where one or both reactants are in low concentrations, the particles are spread out – the particles will collide with each other less often resulting in fewer successful collisions.	Where there are high concentrations of one or both reactants, the particles are crowded close together – the particles will collide with each other more often, resulting in many more successful collisions.

We see a similar effect when the reactants are gases. As the pressure on a gas is increased, the particles are pushed closer together so they collide more often and the reaction is faster.

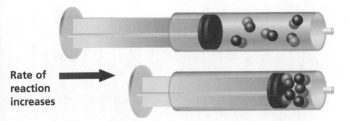

Rate of reaction increases

HT **Concentrations** of solutions are given in **moles per cubic decimetre (mol/dm³)**. Equal volumes of solutions of the same molar concentration contain the same number of moles of solute, i.e. the same number of particles.

Equal volumes of gases at the same temperature and pressure contain the same number of molecules.

Surface Area of Solid Reactants

Large particles have a small surface area in relation to their volume, so fewer particles are exposed and available for collisions. This means fewer collisions and a slower reaction. Small particles have a large surface area in relation to their volume, so more particles are exposed and available for collisions. This means more collisions and a faster reaction.

Large Particles	Small Particles
• Small surface area. • Fewer collisions. • Reaction rate is slow.	• Large surface area. • More collisions. • Reaction rate is faster.

Using a Catalyst

A **catalyst** is a substance which increases the rate of a chemical reaction without being used up or altered in the process. It can be used over and over again to increase the rate at which reactants are converted into products.

A catalyst lowers the amount of energy needed for a successful collision, so more collisions will be successful and the reaction will be faster. Also, it provides a surface for the molecules to attach to, thereby increasing their chances of bumping into each other.

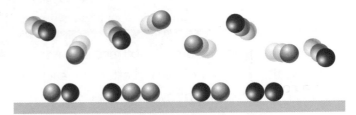

Catalysts are specific to reactions, i.e. different reactions need different catalysts, e.g. the cracking of hydrocarbons uses broken pottery; the manufacture of ammonia (Haber process) uses iron.

Increasing the rates of chemical reactions is important in industry because it helps to reduce costs.

Catalysts used in the cracking of hydrocarbons

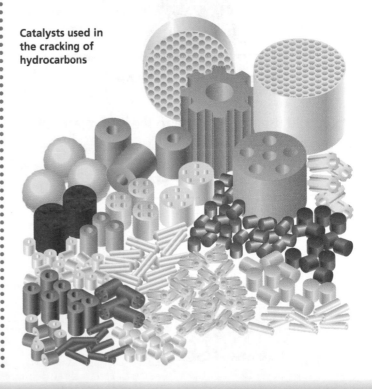

Chemistry Unit 2

Analysing the Rate of Reaction

The rate of a chemical reaction can be found by…
- measuring the amount of reactants used
- measuring the amount of products formed.

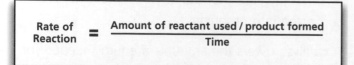

Rate of Reaction	=	Amount of reactant used / product formed
		Time

For example, the decomposition of hydrogen peroxide using manganese (IV) oxide.

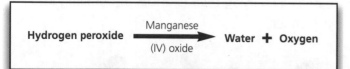

Hydrogen peroxide $\xrightarrow{\text{Manganese (IV) oxide}}$ Water + Oxygen

You could measure the amount of reactant used by weighing the mixture before and after the reaction takes place. In the case of hydrogen peroxide, oxygen is released from the mixture so the mass of the mixture will decrease.

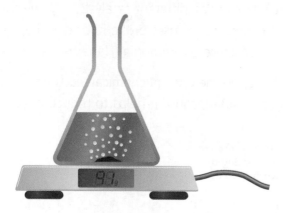

You could use a gas syringe to measure the volume of gas produced, in this case, oxygen.

To test for oxygen gas, insert a glowing splint into a jar of collected gas. Oxygen will relight a glowing splint.

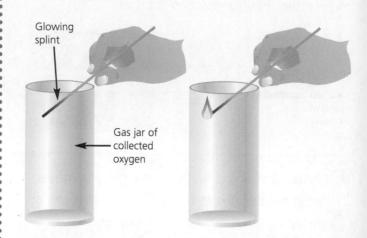

Glowing splint

Gas jar of collected oxygen

Graphs can then be plotted to show the progress of a chemical reaction – there are three things to remember…

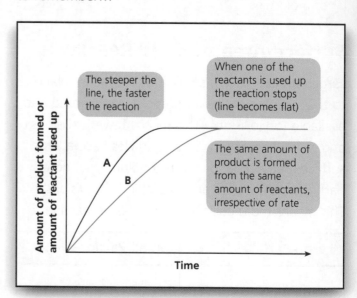

The steeper the line, the faster the reaction

When one of the reactants is used up the reaction stops (line becomes flat)

The same amount of product is formed from the same amount of reactants, irrespective of rate

Amount of product formed or amount of reactant used up

A

B

Time

Reaction **A** is faster than reaction **B**. This could be because…
- the surface area of the solid reactants in **A** is greater than in **B**
- the temperature of reaction **A** is greater than reaction **B**
- the concentration of the solution in **A** is greater than in **B**
- a catalyst is used in reaction **A** but not in reaction **B**.

How Science Works

You need to be able to interpret graphs showing the amount of product formed (or reactant used up) with time, in terms of the rate of the reaction.

The rate of a reaction is the amount of reactant used up or product made, in a given time. One of the factors which affects the rate of reaction is: the concentration of dissolved reactants.

An investigation was carried out to find out how different concentrations of hydrochloric acid affect the rate of reaction between marble chips and hydrochloric acid. The reaction which takes place is:

Calcium carbonate + Dilute hydrochloric acid ➡ Calcium chloride + Carbon dioxide + Water

$$CaCO_{3(s)} + 2HCl_{(aq)} \longrightarrow CaCl_{2(aq)} + CO_{2(g)} + H_2O_{(l)}$$

The table below shows how the acid was diluted.

Volume of acid (cm³)	Volume of water (cm³)	Graph number
0	50	No reaction
10	40	1
20	30	2
30	20	3
40	10	4
50	0	5

Each of the reactions were started and readings of the volume of carbon dioxide gas produced were taken continuously over 10 minutes. The volume was recorded every 30 seconds. This method of collecting results or data is called a continuous method. This method measures the rate of the product made.

A graph was plotted of the volume of carbon dioxide produced against time for each concentration of the hydrochloric acid.

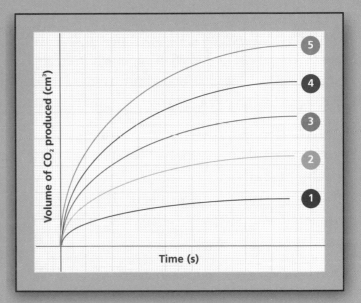

The rate of reaction can be worked out from the graphs. We can see that the most concentrated solution (graph 5) has the steepest curve on the graph, which means it produced CO_2 the quickest. Graph 1 shows the least steep curve which tells us that this reaction was the slowest at producing CO_2.

How Science Works

You need to be able to explain and evaluate the development, advantages and disadvantages of using catalysts in industrial processes.

Catalysts are substances which speed up the rate of a reaction whilst remaining chemically unchanged and without being used up, which means they can be used repeatedly.

As this makes the reaction faster, and the product is produced more quickly, this can save an enormous amount of money in labour and energy costs. Greater quantities of the product can then be made quickly to meet further demand.

Catalysts can be used to get the reaction to take place at lower temperatures, which means less activation energy is needed. This makes it easier for the reaction to start and reduces the energy requirements of the process which is good for sustainable development and also reduces cost.

Catalysts have been used in industrial processes for years. Different reactions require different catalysts so a number of catalysts have been developed.

Many transition metals are used, e.g. iron is used in the production of ammonia, platinum in the production of nitric acid, and silica / aluminium oxide in the production of alkenes (which make plastics).

As technology has become more advanced, scientists are able to work with smaller and smaller structures, such as nanomaterials. Their very, very small size means they have a large surface area in relation to their size, which makes them ideal to be used as industrial catalysts.

However, it is important to remember that different reactions require different catalysts and they are very expensive to buy. They also need to be removed from the product and cleaned regularly otherwise they become 'poisoned' and will not work properly.

The table alongside lists the advantages and disadvantages of using catalysts.

Nanomaterials used as industrial catalysts

Advantages

- They increase the rate of reaction which speeds up industrial processes.
- They reduce the costs of industrial processes.
- They save energy.
- They help sustainable development.
- They can be used over and over again.

Disadvantages

- They are expensive.
- They need to be cleaned regularly to prevent them becoming poisoned.

12.5

Do chemical reactions always release energy?

Chemical reactions either take in or give out energy. Energy requirements and emissions need to be carefully considered in industry. To understand this, you need to know…

- what the terms 'exothermic' and 'endothermic' mean
- how equilibrium can be reached in a reversible reaction
- that the yield depends on the conditions of the reaction.

When chemical reactions occur, energy is transferred to or from the surroundings, so many chemical reactions are accompanied by a temperature change.

Exothermic Reactions

These reactions are accompanied by a temperature rise. They are known as **exothermic** reactions because they transfer heat energy to the surroundings, i.e. they give out heat. Combustion is a common example of an exothermic reaction, e.g.

Methane (natural gas)	+ Oxygen	$\longrightarrow$	Carbon dioxide	+ Water	+ Heat energy
CH_4	$+ 2O_2$	$\longrightarrow$	CO_2	$+ 2H_2O$	

It is not only reactions between fuels and oxygen which are exothermic. Neutralising alkalis with acids gives out heat too, as do many oxidation reactions.

> **HT** If the temperature is raised, the yield decreases. If the temperature is lowered, the yield increases.

Endothermic Reactions

These reactions are accompanied by a fall in temperature. They are known as **endothermic** reactions because heat energy is transferred from the surroundings, i.e. they take in heat. Dissolving ammonium nitrate crystals in water is an endothermic reaction…

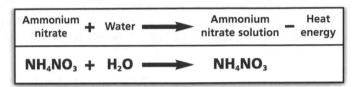

Ammonium nitrate	+ Water	$\longrightarrow$	Ammonium nitrate solution	− Heat energy
NH_4NO_3	$+ H_2O$	$\longrightarrow$	NH_4NO_3	

Thermal decomposition is also an example of an endothermic reaction.

> **HT** If the temperature is raised, the yield increases. If the temperature is lowered, the yield decreases.

Gaseous Reactions

In gaseous reactions, an increase in pressure favours the reaction which produces the least number of molecules.

*N.B. These factors above, along with reaction rates, determine the optimum conditions in industrial processes. An important example is the **Haber process** (see page 56).*

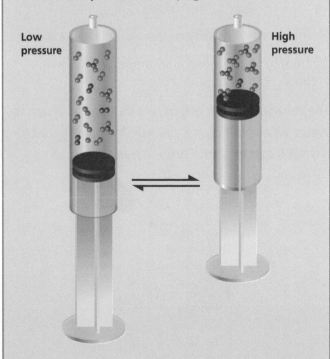

Low pressure

High pressure

Chemistry Unit 2

Reversible Reactions

If a reaction is reversible and it is exothermic in one direction then it follows that it is endothermic in the opposite direction, with the same amount of energy being transferred in each case. An example of this is when hydrated copper sulfate is gently heated.

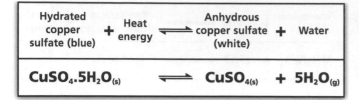

If water is added to white anhydrous copper sulfate, blue hydrated copper sulfate is formed as heat is given out.

Blue crystals of hydrated copper sulfate become white anhydrous copper sulfate on heating, as water is removed.

The reverse reaction above can be used as a test for water where the colour change from white to blue is an indication of the presence of water.

Reversible Reactions in Closed Systems

When a reversible reaction occurs in a closed system (where no reactants are added and no products are removed) then an equilibrium is achieved where the reactions occur at exactly the same rate in both directions. The relative amounts of all the reacting substances at equilibrium depend on the conditions of the reaction. If we take the reaction...

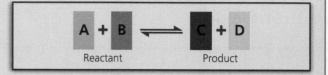

If the forward reaction (the reaction that produces the products C and D) is endothermic then...

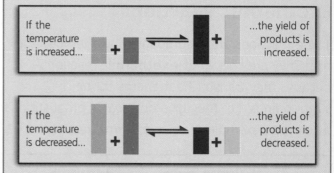

If the forward reaction is exothermic then...

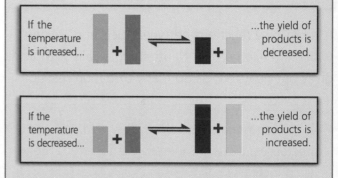

Even though a reversible reaction may not go to completion, it may still be used efficiently in an industrial process, e.g. the Haber process (see p.56).

Sustainable Development

It is important for sustainable development and economic reasons to minimise energy use and wastage in industrial processes.

Non-vigorous conditions mean less energy is used and less is released into the environment, but the reaction is less efficient.

Effect of Varying Conditions on Reversible Reactions

The manufacture of ammonia is a reversible reaction, involving energy transfers associated with the breaking and formation of chemical bonds.

$$N_2 + 3H_2 \underset{\text{Endothermic}}{\overset{\text{Exothermic}}{\rightleftharpoons}} 2NH_3$$

Less energy is needed to break the bonds between the nitrogen and hydrogen molecules than is released in the formation of the ammonia molecules.

Effect of Temperature

At low temperatures, the production of ammonia (the forward reaction), which is an exothermic reaction, is favoured, i.e. the yield of ammonia is increased.

Increasing the temperature increases the rate of reaction equally in both directions, therefore high temperatures make ammonia form faster, but also break down faster.

Effect of Pressure

Increasing the pressure favours the smaller volume. Therefore high pressure favours the production of ammonia, since four molecules are being changed into two molecules, and increases the yield.

A Compromise Solution

Altering the temperature and pressure can have a big impact on the production of ammonia in the Haber process. The conditions have to be chosen very carefully to be economically viable and to make sure they can meet demand.

The formation of ammonia is exothermic so a low temperature increases the yield, but the reaction is very slow. A high temperature makes the reaction faster, but produces a lower yield. So a compromise is reached.

The volume of ammonia produced is less than the total volume of the reactants (nitrogen and hydrogen) so a high pressure favours the production of ammonia, but this is very expensive. A low pressure is more affordable, but this produces a low yield. So yet again a compromise is reached.

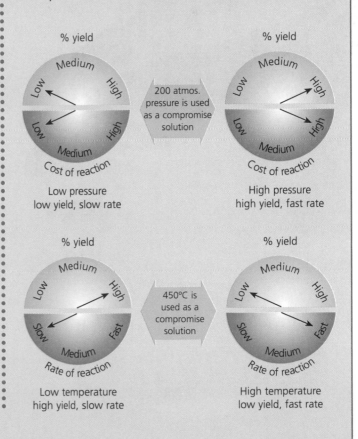

Low pressure
low yield, slow rate

200 atmos. pressure is used as a compromise solution

High pressure
high yield, fast rate

Low temperature
high yield, slow rate

450°C is used as a compromise solution

High temperature
low yield, fast rate

How Science Works

You need to be able to evaluate the conditions used in industrial processes in terms of energy requirements.

Chemical reactions involve energy transfers. Many chemical reactions involve the release of energy and some reactions take in energy. In industrial processes, energy requirements and emissions need to be considered both for economic reasons and for sustainable development. It is important that energy is not wasted in industrial processes. Non-vigorous conditions mean less energy is used and less is lost into the environment.

The conditions used in any industrial process must be considered in terms of the yield of the product. There might need to be a compromise between maximum yield and speed of reaction.

It could be more economical to wait longer for the sake of a higher yield.

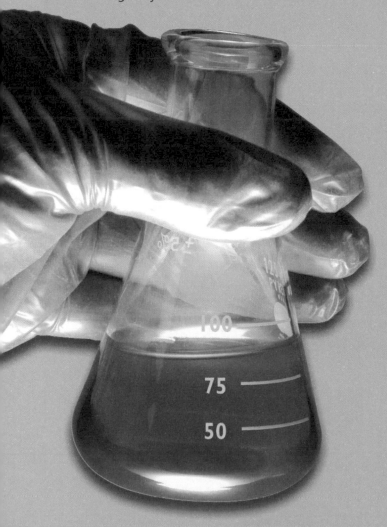

Using a catalyst

Adding a catalyst lowers the activation energy for a reaction so lower temperatures can be used. This usually results in a saving in energy costs.

Changing Pressure or Temperature

Raising the temperature in a chemical reaction increases the energy of the particles involved and they move faster. If they move faster more collisions between the particles take place and this means the reaction goes faster. Sometimes, however, the higher temperature can encourage some of the products made to break up and so this is not favourable to the forward reaction. A compromise temperature is then chosen for the process to proceed at.

Increasing the pressure also increases the reaction because the particles have less room to spread out in, so they collide much more often.

When evaluating the methods used in industry, we need to take into account the amount of energy needed for a reaction, the percentage yield that each method makes, the cost, and the impact on the environment.

Using a Catalyst

Advantages
- Reduces activation energy needed for a reaction.
- Speeds up reaction.
- Reduces cost of reaction.

Disadvantages
- Different reactions need different catalysts.
- Catalyst needs to be removed and cleaned regularly to prevent it from becoming poisoned.
- Purchasing catalysts can be costly.

Increasing Pressure or Temperature

Advantages
- Increases rate of reaction.
- May get a higher percentage yield.

Disadvantages
- Reaction would cost more.
- Percentage yield will only increase up to a certain point.

12.6

How can we use ions in solutions?

Ionic compounds can be used in electrolysis to produce many useful products. Oxidation-reduction reactions involve the transfer of electrons. Ionic solutions can be used to make soluble and insoluble salts. To understand this, you need to know…

- the state symbols
- the properties of ions in solutions
- about electrolysis and its uses
- how to make soluble and insoluble salts
- what the pH scale measures.

State Symbols

The states of the compounds and elements involved in reactions are shown using the state symbols: (s) solid, (l) liquid, (aq) aqueous and (g) gas. An aqueous solution is produced when a substance is dissolved in water.

Electrolysis

Electrolysis is the breaking down of a compound containing ions (charged particles) into its elements using an electrical current. During electrolysis, ions gain or lose electrons at the electrodes, forming electrically neutral atoms or molecules which are then released (i.e. they have no charge).

Principles of Electrolysis

Ionic substances are chemical compounds that allow an electric current to flow through them when they are molten or dissolved in water.

These compounds contain negative and positive ions and the electric current is due to negatively charged ions moving to the positive electrode and positively charged ions moving to the negative electrode. When this happens, simpler substances are released at the two electrodes. This is **electrolysis**.

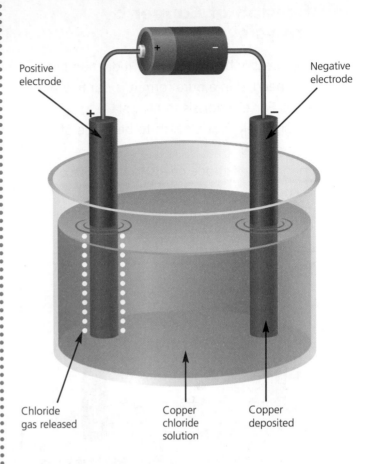

Positive electrode

Negative electrode

Chloride gas released

Copper chloride solution

Copper deposited

If there is a mixture of ions in the solution, the products formed depend on the reactivity of the elements involved. For example, in the electrolysis of copper chloride solution, the simple substances released are copper at the negative electrode and chlorine gas at the positive electrode.

Redox Reactions

During electrolysis, positively charged ions gain electrons at the negative electrode. This gain of electrons is known as **reduction**.

At the positive electrode, negatively charged ions lose electrons. This loss of electrons is known as **oxidation**.

A chemical reaction where both reduction and oxidation occurs is called a **redox** reaction. It will help you to remember the above if you remember the word **oilrig**.

- **O**xidation **I**s **L**oss of electrons (**OIL**)
- **R**eduction **I**s **G**ain of electrons (**RIG**)

Chemistry Unit 2

Purification of Copper by Electrolysis

Copper can easily be extracted by reduction but when it is needed in a pure form it is purified by electrolysis. For electrolysis to take place...

- the positive electrode needs to be made of impure copper
- the negative electrode needs to be made of pure copper
- the solution must contain copper ions.

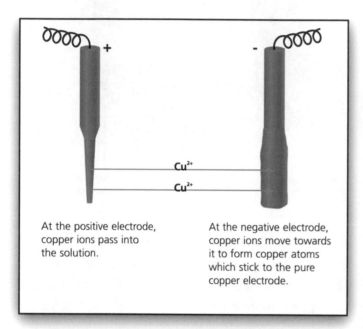

At the positive electrode, copper ions pass into the solution.

At the negative electrode, copper ions move towards it to form copper atoms which stick to the pure copper electrode.

Consequently, the negative electrode gets bigger and bigger as the positive electrode seems to dissolve away to nothing. The impurities in the positive electrode simply fall to the bottom as the process takes place.

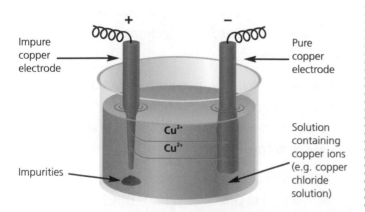

Impure copper electrode

Pure copper electrode

Impurities

Solution containing copper ions (e.g. copper chloride solution)

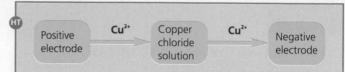

HT

Positive electrode → Cu^{2+} → Copper chloride solution → Cu^{2+} → Negative electrode

The reactions that occur at the electrodes can be represented by half-equations. When you write the half-equations of the reactions that occur at the electrodes, remember to include the state symbols: (s) solid, (l) liquid, (aq) aqueous, (g) gas.

The following half-equations show the reactions that occur at the electrodes during the electrolysis of copper. Remember that chlorine exists as molecules.

At the negative electrode:

$$Cu^{2+} + 2e^- \longrightarrow Cu_{(s)}$$

At the positive electrode:

$$2Cl^- \longrightarrow Cl_{2(g)} + 2e^-$$

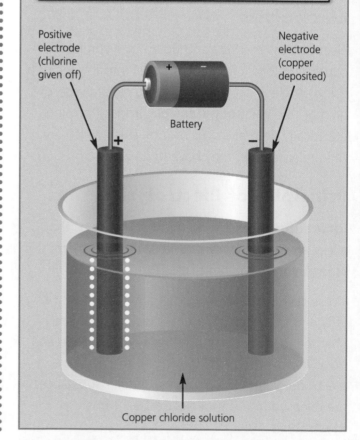

Positive electrode (chlorine given off)

Negative electrode (copper deposited)

Battery

Copper chloride solution

Industrial Electrolysis of Sodium Chloride Solution (Brine)

Sodium chloride (common salt) is a compound of an alkali metal and a halogen. It is found in large quantities in the sea and in underground deposits. Electrolysis of sodium chloride solution produces some very important reagents for the chemical industry…

- chlorine gas at the positive electrode
- hydrogen gas at the negative electrode
- sodium hydroxide solution which is passed out of the cell.

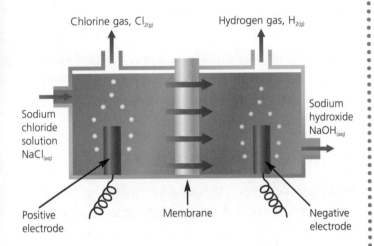

The products of the electrolysis of brine have many uses…

- chlorine is used to kill bacteria in drinking water and swimming pools and to manufacture hydrochloric acid, disinfectants, bleach and the plastic PVC
- hydrogen is used in the manufacture of ammonia and margarine
- sodium hydroxide is used in the manufacture of soap, paper and ceramics.

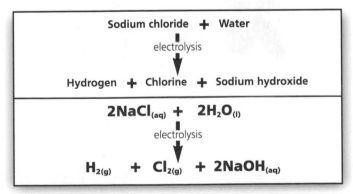

A simple laboratory test for chlorine is that it bleaches damp litmus paper, i.e. the chlorine removes the colour.

Indicators

Indicators are useful dyes which change colour depending on whether they are in acidic or alkaline solutions.

Some are simple substances such as litmus, which changes from red to blue or vice versa. Others are mixtures of dyes, such as universal indicator, which show a range of colour to indicate just how acidic or alkaline a substance is.

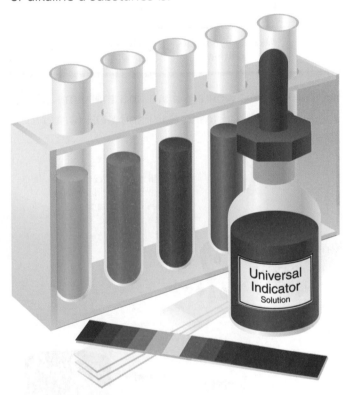

pH Scale

The pH scale is a measure of the acidity or alkalinity of an aqueous solution, across a 14 point scale.

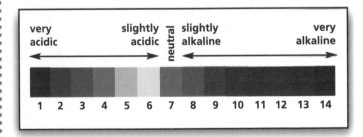

When substances dissolve in water, they dissociate into their individual ions…

- hydroxide ions ($OH^-_{(aq)}$) make solutions alkaline
- hydrogen ions ($H^+_{(aq)}$) make solutions acidic.

Chemistry Unit 2

Neutralisation

Acids and alkalis are **chemical opposites**, so if they are added together in the correct amounts they can 'cancel' each other out. This is because the hydrogen ions react with hydroxide ions to produce water.

This is called neutralisation because the solution which remains has a neutral pH of 7.

We can see this working if we add the same volumes of HCl (a strong acid) and KOH (a strong alkali) together.

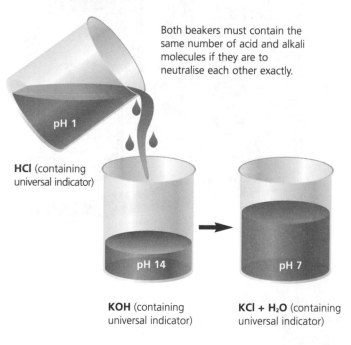

Both beakers must contain the same number of acid and alkali molecules if they are to neutralise each other exactly.

HCl (containing universal indicator)

KOH (containing universal indicator)

KCl + H₂O (containing universal indicator)

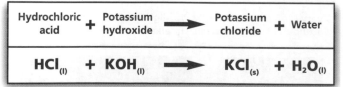

Again, if we look at what happens to the hydrogen ions $H^+_{(aq)}$ and the hydroxide ions $OH^-_{(aq)}$ in the acid and alkali, we can see that they react to form water...

$$H^+_{(aq)} + OH^-_{(aq)} \longrightarrow H_2O_{(l)}$$

Ammonia is an alkaline gas which dissolves in water to make an alkaline solution. Its main use is in the production of fertilisers to increase the nitrogen content of the soil. Ammonia neutralises nitric acid to produce ammonium nitrate (a fertiliser rich in nitrogen), which is sometimes known as 'nitram' (nitrate of ammonia). The aqueous ammonium nitrate is then evaporated to dryness.

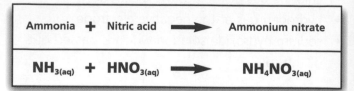

Nitrogen-based fertilisers are important chemicals as they increase the yields of crops. However, nitrates can create problems if they find their way into streams, rivers or groundwater, as they can upset the natural balance and contaminate our drinking water.

Soluble Salts from Metals

Metals which react with dilute acid form a metal salt and hydrogen. **Salt** is a word used to describe any metal compound made when a reaction takes place between a metal and an acid.

However, some metals react more vigorously than others...

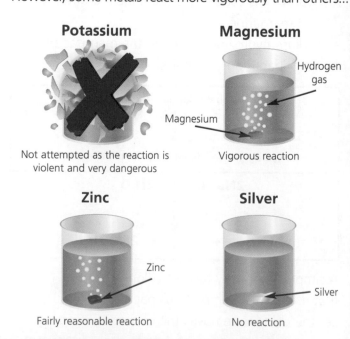

Soluble Salts from Insoluble Bases

Bases are the oxides and hydroxides of metals. Those which are soluble are called **alkalis**.

Unfortunately, the oxides and hydroxides of transition metals are insoluble, which means that preparing their salts is a little less straightforward.

The metal oxide or hydroxide is added to an acid until no more will react. The excess metal oxide or hydroxide is then filtered off to leave a solution of the salt which can then be evaporated to dryness.

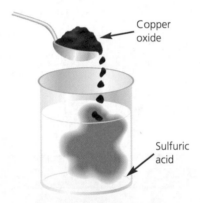

Add copper oxide to sulfuric acid

Filter to remove any unreacted copper oxide

Evaporate to leave behind blue crystals of the 'salt' copper sulfate

| Sulfuric acid | + | Copper oxide | → | Copper sulfate | + | Water |

This can be written more generally as…

| Acid | + | Base | → | Neutral salt solution | + | Water |

Ammonia also dissolves in water to produce an alkaline solution. This can be neutralised with acids to produce ammonium salts (see p.70), which are important as fertilisers.

	Hydrochloric acid	Sulfuric acid	Nitric acid
Ammonium hydroxide	Ammonium chloride and water	Ammonium sulfate and water	Ammonium nitrate and water

Salts of Alkali Metals

Compounds of alkali metals, called salts, can be made by reacting solutions of their hydroxides (which are alkaline) with a particular acid. This is called a neutralisation reaction (see p.70) and can be represented as follows…

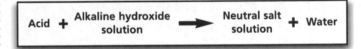

| Acid | + | Alkaline hydroxide solution | → | Neutral salt solution | + | Water |

The salt produced depends on the metal in the alkali and the acid used.

	Hydrochloric acid	Sulfuric acid	Nitric acid
Sodium hydroxide	Sodium chloride and water	Sodium sulfate and water	Sodium nitrate and water
Potassium hydroxide	Potassium chloride and water	Potassium sulfate and water	Potassium nitrate and water

Insoluble Salts

Insoluble salts can be made by mixing appropriate solutions of ions so that a solid substance (precipitate) is formed. Precipitation can be used to remove unwanted ions from solution, e.g. softening hard water. The calcium (or magnesium) ions are precipitated out as insoluble calcium (or magnesium) carbonate.

How Science Works

You need to be able to predict the results of electrolysing solutions of ions.

Ionic substances conduct electricity and can be broken down when they are molten or in solution. The process of electrolysis uses electrical energy to break down these substances and is used to manufacture important chemical substances that we use in our everyday lives.

The following rules can be used to predict the results of electrolysing solutions.

- If a metal is high in the Reactivity series, hydrogen is produced at the negative electrode instead of the metal.
- If the metal is below hydrogen in the Reactivity series, the metal is produced.
- If you have concentrated solutions of chlorides, bromides or iodides then chlorine, bromine or iodine is produced at the positive electrode. With other common negative ions oxygen is produced.

HT **You need to be able to complete and balance supplied half-equations for the reactions occurring at the electrodes during electrolysis.**

We can write and balance half-equations to show what happens at each electrode during the electrolysis. For example, for the electrolysis of brine (salt water). Write down a word equation…

Sodium chloride + Water $\xrightarrow{\text{electrolysis}}$ Sodium hydroxide + Chlorine + Hydrogen

$$2NaCl + 2H_2O \longrightarrow 2NaOH + Cl_2 + H_2$$

Then look at what happens at the positive electrode…

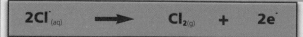

$$2Cl^-_{(aq)} \longrightarrow Cl_{2(g)} + 2e^-$$

… and what happens at the negative electrode…

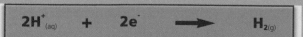

$$2H^+_{(aq)} + 2e^- \longrightarrow H_{2(g)}$$

The sodium ions (Na^+) and the hydroxide ions (OH^-) combine to produce sodium hydroxide (NaOH).

You need to be able to explain and evaluate processes that use the principles described in this unit.

The process of electrolysis uses electrical energy to break down ionic substances, which are molten or in solution, into elements. This process is important industrially as it is used to manufacture important chemical substances we need for our everyday lives.

Example

The electrolysis of sea water or brine (see p.69) gives us large quantities of hydrogen gas, chlorine and sodium hydroxide solution. These products are also used as the starting point for other useful products such as disinfectants, fertilisers and soap.

The process is very expensive because of all the energy which is required to bring about the change.

Advantages

- Three very important materials (hydrogen, chlorine and sodium hydroxide) are produced from one raw material (brine).
- Brine is a renewable source which is readily available and cheap.
- The products of the electrolysis of brine are used in many industries to make a large variety of products.
- As all the products are useful there is a minimum of waste.

Disadvantages

- The process of electrolysis is very expensive as it depends upon electrical energy to work.
- The production of electrical energy in traditional power stations adds to the pollution in the atmosphere.
- Hydrogen and chlorine can be produced by other methods much more cheaply.

You need to be able to suggest methods to make a named salt.

Example

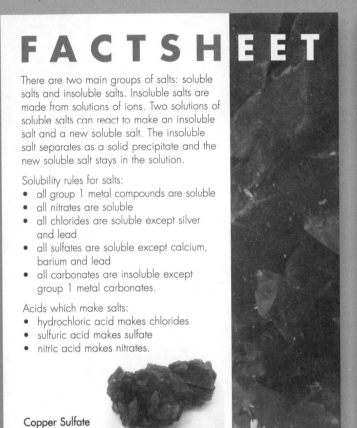

FACTSHEET

There are two main groups of salts: soluble salts and insoluble salts. Insoluble salts are made from solutions of ions. Two solutions of soluble salts can react to make an insoluble salt and a new soluble salt. The insoluble salt separates as a solid precipitate and the new soluble salt stays in the solution.

Solubility rules for salts:
- all group 1 metal compounds are soluble
- all nitrates are soluble
- all chlorides are soluble except silver and lead
- all sulfates are soluble except calcium, barium and lead
- all carbonates are insoluble except group 1 metal carbonates.

Acids which make salts:
- hydrochloric acid makes chlorides
- sulfuric acid makes sulfate
- nitric acid makes nitrates.

Copper Sulfate

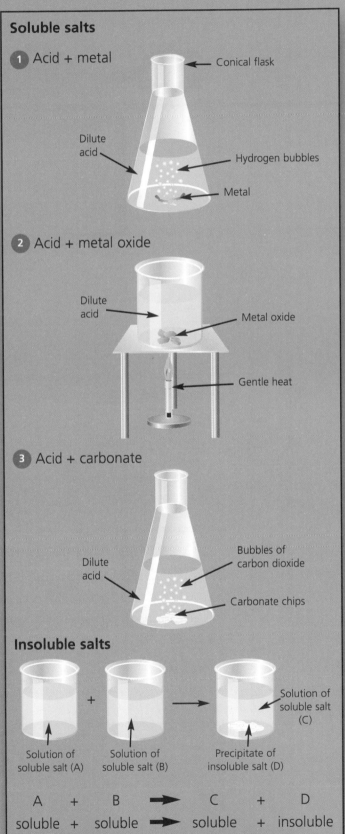

Soluble salts

1 Acid + metal
- Conical flask
- Dilute acid
- Hydrogen bubbles
- Metal

2 Acid + metal oxide
- Dilute acid
- Metal oxide
- Gentle heat

3 Acid + carbonate
- Dilute acid
- Bubbles of carbon dioxide
- Carbonate chips

Insoluble salts
- Solution of soluble salt (A)
- Solution of soluble salt (B)
- Precipitate of insoluble salt (D)
- Solution of soluble salt (C)

A + B → C + D

soluble + soluble → soluble + insoluble

Using the information above, suggest which method (shown right) you would use to make copper sulfate and silver chloride and explain your reasoning.

Copper sulfate is a soluble salt. Copper will not react with acid as it is an unreactive metal. The salt cannot be made from the metal and acid, so we can use the metal oxide and acid. Sulfuric acid makes sulfates.

The excess solid is then filtered off and the solution of copper sulphate is heated gently to evaporate some of the water. The concentrated solution is then left to crystallise.

Silver chloride is an insoluble salt. The method to make silver chloride will use the soluble salt silver nitrate and the soluble salt sodium chloride. Add the two soluble salts together and the insoluble silver chloride will precipitate. The insoluble precipitate can be removed from the solution of sodium nitrate by filtration. The precipitate is then left to dry at room temperature.

Example Questions

For Chemistry Unit 2, you will have to complete one
written paper with structured questions.

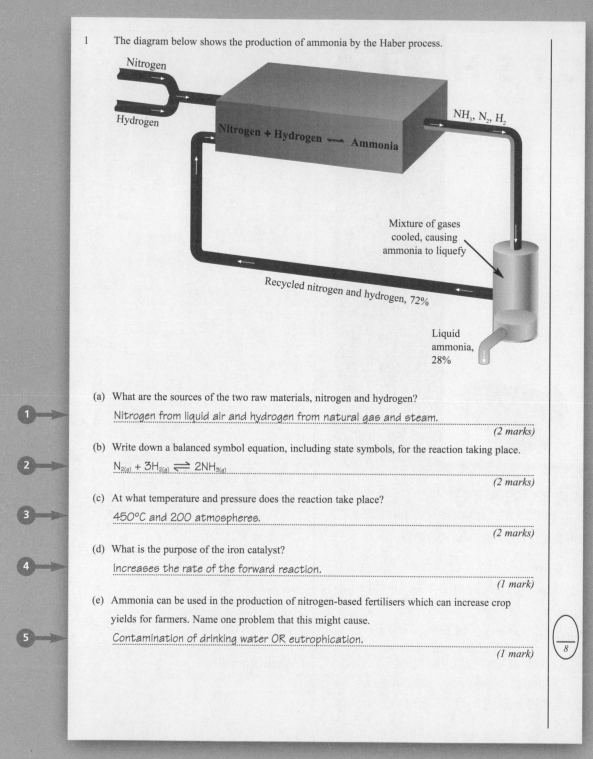

1   The diagram below shows the production of ammonia by the Haber process.

Nitrogen

Hydrogen

Nitrogen + Hydrogen ⇌ Ammonia

NH_3, N_2, H_2

Mixture of gases
cooled, causing
ammonia to liquefy

Recycled nitrogen and hydrogen, 72%

Liquid
ammonia,
28%

(a) What are the sources of the two raw materials, nitrogen and hydrogen?

Nitrogen from liquid air and hydrogen from natural gas and steam.

(2 marks)

(b) Write down a balanced symbol equation, including state symbols, for the reaction taking place.

$N_{2(g)} + 3H_{2(g)} \rightleftharpoons 2NH_{3(g)}$

(2 marks)

(c) At what temperature and pressure does the reaction take place?

450°C and 200 atmospheres.

(2 marks)

(d) What is the purpose of the iron catalyst?

Increases the rate of the forward reaction.

(1 mark)

(e) Ammonia can be used in the production of nitrogen-based fertilisers which can increase crop
yields for farmers. Name one problem that this might cause.

Contamination of drinking water OR eutrophication.

(1 mark)

8

① The wording of the question, and the number of marks available,
clearly tell you how much information you need to give.
② Read the question carefully. You could lose marks here if you forget
the state symbols.

③ Don't forget to include units (e.g. °C) for all measurements!
④ You only need to know what a catalyst does to answer this question.
⑤ The question only requires one example, but there are several
possible answers.

Acid – a compound that has a pH value of lower than 7

Alkali – a compound that has a pH value higher than 7

Alkali metals – elements in Group 1 of the periodic table – lithium, sodium, potassium, rubidium, caesium and francium

Atomic number – the number of protons an element has in the nucleus of its atom; the mass of an atom compared to the mass of a hydrogen atom

Covalent bonding – a bond between two atoms in which both atoms share one electron

Electrodes – pieces of metal or carbon which allow electric current to enter and leave during electrolysis

Electrolysis – the process by which an electric current causes a solution to undergo chemical decomposition

Electron – a negatively charged particle found outside the nucleus of an atom

Endothermic reaction – a reaction which takes in heat from the surroundings

Equilibrium – the state in which a chemical reaction proceeds at the same rate as its reverse reaction

Exothermic reaction – a reaction which gives off heat

Halogens – elements in Group 7 of the periodic table – fluorine, chlorine, bromine, iodine and astatine

Ionic bonding – the process by which two or more atoms lose or gain electrons to become charged ions

Mole (mol) – the molar mass of a substance, i.e. the mass in grammes of 6×10^{23} particles

Nanomaterials – materials with a very small grain size

Neutralisation – reaction between an acid and a base which forms a neutral solution

Neutron – a particle found in the nucleus of atoms that has no electric charge

Noble gas – an inert, colourless gas, e.g. helium, neon, krypton, xenon or radon

Nucleus – the small central core of an atom, consisting of protons and neutrons

Oxidation – a reaction involving the gain of oxygen or the loss of hydrogen

Precipitation – the removal of particles from a solution

Proton – a positively charged particle found in the nucleus of atoms

Reduction – a reaction involving the loss of oxygen or the gain of hydrogen

Relative atomic mass (A_r) – The average mass of the isotopes of a particular element compared to the ^{12}C isotope

Relative formula mass (M_r) – the sum of the atomic masses of all atoms in a molecule

Reversible reaction – a reaction in which products react to reform the original reactants

Salt – the product of a chemical reaction between a base and an acid

Smart materials – materials that have one or more properties that can be altered

Yield – the amount of a product obtained from a reaction

Physics Unit 2

13.1

How can we describe the way things move?

Movement is not easy to describe. Objects can move at different speeds and in different directions. Distance–time graphs and velocity–time graphs can help to describe movement. To understand this, you need to know…

- what speed, acceleration and velocity are
- how to calculate acceleration
- how a distance–time graph represents speed
- how a velocity–time graph represents acceleration and distance travelled.

Speed

One way of describing the movement of an object is by measuring its **speed**, i.e. how fast it is moving. Since this cyclist travels a distance of 8 metres every 1 second we can say that the speed of the cyclist is 8 metres per second (m/s).

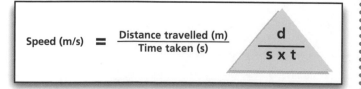

If we want to work out the speed of any moving object we need to know two things:

- the distance it travels
- the time it takes to travel that distance.

We can then calculate the speed of the object using the following formula…

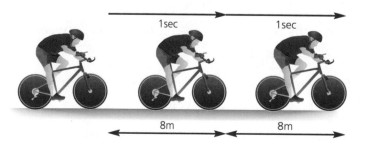

$$\text{Speed (m/s)} = \frac{\text{Distance travelled (m)}}{\text{Time taken (s)}}$$

Speed can also be measured in kilometres per hour (km/h) and miles per hour (mph).

Example

Calculate the speed of a cyclist who travels 2400m in 5 minutes.

$$\text{Speed (m/s)} = \frac{\text{Distance travelled (m)}}{\text{Time taken (s)}} = \frac{2400}{300} = \textbf{8m/s}$$

Multiply 5 minutes by 60 to get time in seconds

Distance–Time Graphs

The slope of a **distance–time graph** represents the speed of an object; the steeper the slope, the greater the speed.

Stationary object: 'y' axis shows distance from a fixed point (0), not total distance travelled.

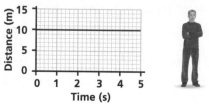

Object is moving at a constant speed of 2m/s.

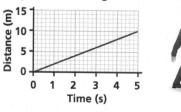

$$\frac{10}{5} = \textbf{2m/s}$$

Object is moving at a greater constant speed of 3m/s.

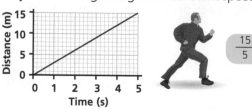

$$\frac{15}{5} = \textbf{3m/s}$$

Velocity

Velocity and speed are not the same thing. The velocity of a moving object describes its speed in a given direction, i.e. the speed and the direction of travel are both known.

Velocity of the car is 40km/h East

Velocity of the car is 40km/h South

Acceleration

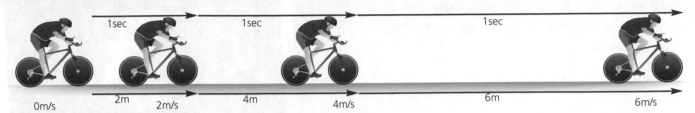

0m/s 2m 2m/s 4m 4m/s 6m 6m/s

1sec 1sec 1sec

The **acceleration** of an object is the rate at which its velocity changes. In other words it is a measure of how quickly an object speeds up or slows down.

The cyclist above increases his velocity by 2 metres per second every second. So, we can say that his acceleration is 2m/s² (2 metres per second, per second). To work out the acceleration of any moving object you need to know two things:

* the change in velocity
* the time taken for this change in velocity.

You can then calculate the acceleration of the object using the following formula...

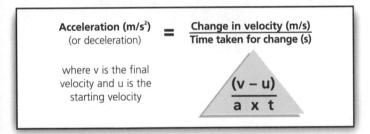

Acceleration (m/s²) (or deceleration) $=$ $\dfrac{\text{Change in velocity (m/s)}}{\text{Time taken for change (s)}}$

where v is the final velocity and u is the starting velocity

$$\frac{(v-u)}{a \times t}$$

There are two important points to be aware of:

1 the cyclist above increases his velocity by the *same amount* every second; the *actual* distance travelled each second increases

2 deceleration is simply a negative acceleration, i.e. it describes an object that is slowing down.

Example

A cyclist accelerates uniformly from rest and reaches a velocity of 10m/s after 5s, then decelerates uniformly and comes to a halt in a further 10s. Calculate **a)** his acceleration, and **b)** his deceleration.

a) Acceleration $= \dfrac{\text{Change in velocity}}{\text{Time taken}}$

$= \dfrac{10-0}{5}$ $= \mathbf{2m/s^2}$

b) Deceleration $= \dfrac{\text{Change in velocity}}{\text{Time taken}}$

$= \dfrac{0-10}{10}$ $= \mathbf{-1m/s^2}$

i.e. a deceleration (make sure you state this)

Velocity–Time Graphs

The slope of a **velocity–time graph** represents the acceleration of the object; the steeper the slope, the greater the acceleration. The area underneath the line in a velocity–time graph represents the total distance travelled.

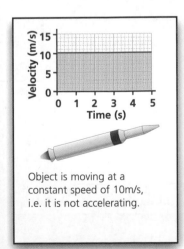

Object is moving at a constant speed of 10m/s, i.e. it is not accelerating.

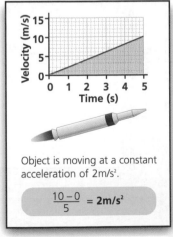

Object is moving at a constant acceleration of 2m/s².

$\dfrac{10-0}{5} = 2m/s^2$

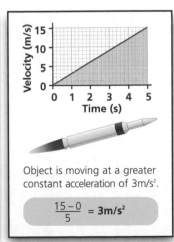

Object is moving at a greater constant acceleration of 3m/s².

$\dfrac{15-0}{5} = 3m/s^2$

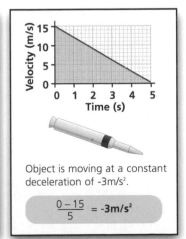

Object is moving at a constant deceleration of -3m/s².

$\dfrac{0-15}{5} = -3m/s^2$

How Science Works

You need to be able to construct distance–time graphs for a body moving in a straight line when the body is stationary or moving with constant speed.

Example

An athlete is training for a marathon. She runs at a constant speed for 1 minute and then rests for 20 seconds to allow her pulse rate to slow down. She repeats this 4 times. For each minute that she is running, she covers 400m. This information can be plotted on a distance–time graph (see below).

The sloping lines show when the athlete is running and the flat lines show when she is stationary. The sloping lines are all at the same angle showing that the athlete was always running at the same speed.

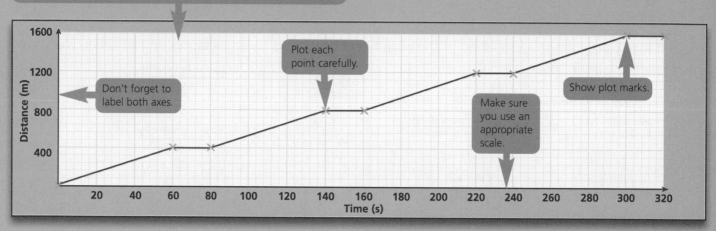

Don't forget to label both axes.

Plot each point carefully.

Make sure you use an appropriate scale.

Show plot marks.

You need to be able to construct velocity–time graphs for a body moving with a constant velocity or a constant acceleration.

The flat lines show where the athlete was running at a constant velocity. The sloping line shows where she increased her speed, accelerating at a constant speed. Graphs like this provide a clear visual representation of data, which can make it much easier to understand.

Example

The same athlete practises a sprint finish by running in a straight line at a constant speed (i.e. velocity) of 7m/s for 20 seconds before gradually increasing her speed to a sprint. It takes her 20 seconds to reach a top speed of 9m/s accelerating at a constant rate. She then maintains this top speed for a further 20 seconds. This information can be plotted on a velocity–time graph (see opposite).

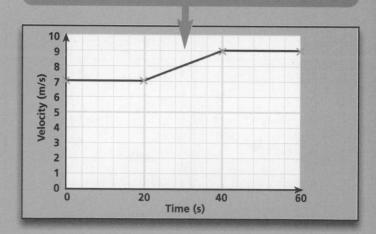

You need to be able to calculate the speed of a body from the slope of a distance–time graph.

Example

Here is a distance–time graph. Calculate the speed of the body during the three parts of the journey using the formula…

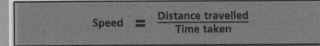

$$\text{Speed} = \frac{\text{Distance travelled}}{\text{Time taken}}$$

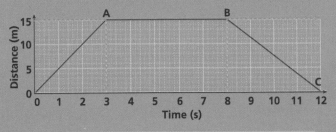

0 to A: Substitute figures into the formula…

Speed from 0 to A = $\dfrac{15m}{3s}$ = **5m/s**

A to B: Object stationary (no slope). Prove this using the formula…

Speed from A to B = $\dfrac{0m}{5s}$ = **0m/s**

B to C: Substitute figures into the formula…

Speed from B to C = $\dfrac{15m}{4s}$ = **3.75m/s**

So, the object travelled at 5m/s for 3 seconds, remained stationary for 5 seconds then travelled at 3.75m/s for 4 seconds back to the starting point.

You need to be able to calculate the acceleration of a body from the slope of a velocity–time graph and the distance travelled from a velocity–time graph.

Example

Here is a velocity–time graph. Calculate the acceleration of the three parts of the journey and the total distance travelled.

$$\text{Acceleration} = \frac{\text{Change in velocity}}{\text{Time taken}}$$

Total distance travelled = Total area under graph

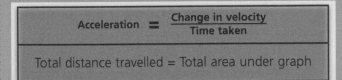

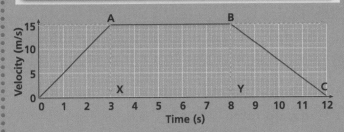

0 to A: Substitute figures into the formula…

Acceleration from 0 to A = $\dfrac{15m/s}{3s}$ = **5m/s²**

A to B: Constant velocity (no slope = no acceleration). Prove this using the formula…

Acceleration from A to B = $\dfrac{0m/s}{5s}$ = **0m/s²**

B to C: Substitute figures into the formula…

Deceleration from B to C = $\dfrac{-15m/s}{4s}$ = **-3.75m/s²**

So, the object accelerated at 5m/s² for 3 seconds, travelled at a constant speed of 15m/s for 5 seconds before decelerating at a rate of -3.75m/s² for 4 seconds.

The total distance travelled can be calculated by working out the area under the velocity–time graph.

= Area of 0AX + Area of ABYX + Area of BCY

= ($\frac{1}{2}$ x 3 x 15) + (5 x 15) + ($\frac{1}{2}$ x 4 x 15) = **127.5m**

Physics Unit 2

13.2

How do we make things speed up or slow down?

To change the speed of an object, an unbalanced force must act on it. To understand this, you need to know…
- what forces act on objects
- the factors that affect the motion of an object
- how force, mass and acceleration are related
- about stopping distances
- what terminal velocity is.

Forces

Forces are pushes or pulls. They are measured in **newtons (N)** and may vary in size and act in different directions.

When a stationary object rests on a surface it exerts a **downward force** (weight). The surface it rests on exerts an **upward force** (reaction). These two forces are equal and opposite and therefore the object remains stationary.

Upward force (reaction)   Downward force (weight)

A number of forces acting on an object can be replaced by a single force which has the same effect on the object as the original forces all acting together. This is called the **resultant force**.

Friction

Friction is a force that occurs when an object moves through a medium, e.g. air or water, or when surfaces slide past each other. It works against the object, in the opposite direction to which it is moving.

When a motor vehicle travels at a steady speed, the frictional forces exactly balance the driving force.

Direction of movement   Friction

Stopping Distance

The stopping distance of a vehicle depends on…
- **the thinking distance** – the distance travelled by the vehicle from the point when the driver realises he / she needs to stop to when he / she actually applies the brakes
- **the braking distance** – the distance travelled by the vehicle from the point when the driver applies the brakes to where the vehicle eventually stops.

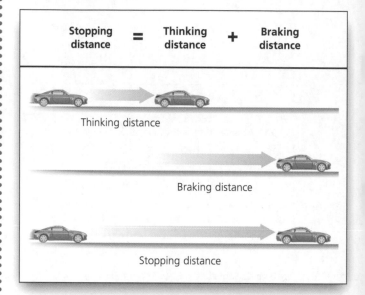

The overall stopping distance is increased if…
- the vehicle is travelling at greater speeds.
  - At 50mph the stopping distance is about 50m, equal to half the length of a football pitch.
  - At 70mph the stopping distance is about 100m, equal to the length of a football pitch.
- there are adverse weather conditions, e.g. wet or icy roads, poor visibility, etc.
  - On a dry road at 50mph the stopping distance is about 50m.
  - On a wet or greasy road at 50mph the stopping distance is about 80m.
- the driver is tired or under the influence of drugs or alcohol and cannot react as quickly as normal
- the vehicle is in a poor condition, e.g. underinflated tyres.

The greater the speed of the vehicle the greater the braking force needed to stop in a certain time.

How Forces Affect Movement

The movement of an object depends on the forces acting upon it.

If they are equal and opposite, the forces acting are balanced. If they are not equal and opposite, then they are unbalanced.

Object	Resultant Forces	
	Zero (Balanced)	**Not Zero (Unbalanced)**
Stationary	• Object remains stationary.	• Object will start to move in the direction of the resultant force.
Moving at a constant speed	• Object will continue at same constant speed in same direction.	• Object will speed up or slow down in the direction of the resultant force.

Example

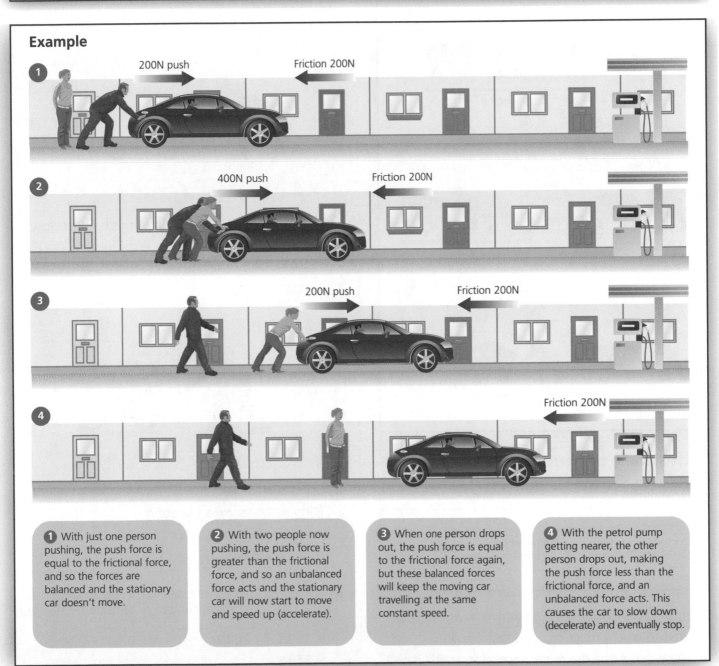

❶ With just one person pushing, the push force is equal to the frictional force, and so the forces are balanced and the stationary car doesn't move.

❷ With two people now pushing, the push force is greater than the frictional force, and so an unbalanced force acts and the stationary car will now start to move and speed up (accelerate).

❸ When one person drops out, the push force is equal to the frictional force again, but these balanced forces will keep the moving car travelling at the same constant speed.

❹ With the petrol pump getting nearer, the other person drops out, making the push force less than the frictional force, and an unbalanced force acts. This causes the car to slow down (decelerate) and eventually stop.

Physics Unit 2

Force, Mass and Acceleration

If an unbalanced force acts on an object then the acceleration of the object will depend on...

- the **size** of the unbalanced force – the bigger the force, the greater the acceleration
- the **mass** of the object – the bigger the mass, the smaller the acceleration.

Example

One boy pushes the trolley, exerting an unbalanced force which causes it to move and accelerate.

Push force

1 second

If two boys push the same trolley it moves with a greater acceleration.

Same mass | Bigger push force | Same mass

1 second

However, if one boy pushes a trolley of bigger mass, it moves with a smaller acceleration than the first trolley.

Bigger mass | Push force | Bigger mass

1 second

The relationship between force, mass and acceleration is shown in the following formula...

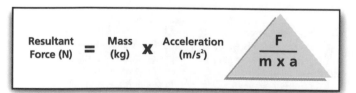

$$\text{Resultant Force (N)} = \text{Mass (kg)} \times \text{Acceleration (m/s}^2)$$

$$\frac{F}{m \times a}$$

From this, we can define a newton (N) as the force needed to give a mass of one kilogram an acceleration of one metre per second squared (1m/s^2).

Example

A trolley of mass 400kg is pushed along a floor with a constant speed by one boy who exerts a push force of 150N.

Another boy joins him to increase the push force and the trolley accelerates at 0.5m/s^2. Calculate...

a) the force needed to achieve this acceleration
b) the total push force exerted on the trolley.

Initially the trolley is moving at a constant speed, so the forces acting on it must be balanced.

Therefore, the 150N push force must be opposed by an equal force, i.e. friction or air resistance.

Constant speed

150N

When the trolley starts accelerating the push force must be greater than friction, etc. These forces do not cancel each other out and an unbalanced force now acts.

Push force

Acceleration of 0.5m/s^2

Friction 150N

a) Using the formula:

Force = Mass x Acceleration
= 400kg x 0.5m/s^2
= **200N**

b) Total push = $\frac{\text{Force needed to}}{\text{equal friction}}$ + $\frac{\text{Force needed to}}{\text{provide acceleration}}$

= 150N + 200N
= **350N**

Terminal Velocity

Falling objects experience two forces...
*   the downward force of weight, W (↓) which always stays the same
*   the upward force of air resistance, R, or drag (↑).

When a skydiver jumps out of an aeroplane, the speed of his descent can be considered in two separate parts:

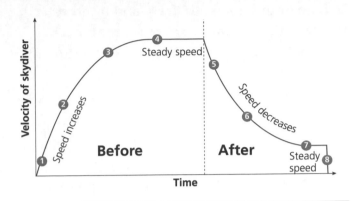

Before the Parachute Opens

When the skydiver jumps, he initially accelerates due to the force of gravity (see **1**). Gravity is a force of attraction that acts between bodies that have mass, e.g. the skydiver and the Earth. The weight of an object is the force exerted on it by gravity. It is measured in newtons (N).

However, as the skydiver falls he experiences the frictional force of air resistance (R) in the opposite direction. But this is not as great as W so he continues to accelerate (see **2**).

As his speed increases, so does the air resistance acting on him (see **3**), until eventually R is equal to W (see **4**). This means that the resultant force acting on him is now zero and his falling speed becomes constant. This speed is called the **terminal velocity**.

After the Parachute Opens

When the parachute is opened, unbalanced forces act again because the upward force of R is now greatly increased and is bigger than W (see **5**). This decreases his speed and as his speed decreases so does R (see **6**).

Eventually R decreases until it is equal to W (see **7**). The forces acting are once again balanced and for the second time he falls at a steady speed, slower than before though, i.e. at a new terminal velocity.

How Science Works

You need to be able to draw and interpret velocity–time graphs for bodies that reach terminal velocity, including a consideration of the forces acting on the body.

Example

An peregrin falcon is flying above the ground at a velocity of 25m/s. After 10 seconds, it spots a mouse on the ground and goes into a vertical dive making itself into a streamlined shape. It takes 15 seconds for the bird to reach a terminal velocity of 95m/s. It then sustains terminal velocity for 5 seconds. This information can be plotted on a velocity–time graph…

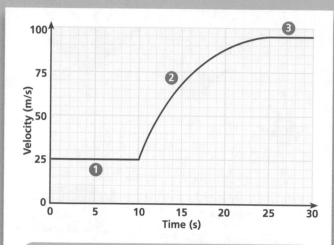

1 The flat line at the start of the graph shows the bird flying at a constant velocity.

2 The curve of the graph begins when the bird enters the dive. The line is steep at first showing fast acceleration. The line gradually becomes less steep because the air resistance acting against the bird slows down acceleration.

3 The flat line at the top of the graph shows the bird has reached terminal velocity and is travelling through the air at a constant velocity.

You need to be able to calculate the weight of a body using the following formula…

| Weight (Newton, N) | = | Mass (Kilogram, kg) | X | Gravitational force strength (Newton/kilogram, N/kg) |

Gravitational field strength is the force that acts on a 1kg mass at a point in a gravitational field. It is measured in newtons per kilogram (N/kg).

Example

The Earth's surface has a gravitational field strength of approximately 10N/kg. The Moon has a gravitational field strength approximately $\frac{1}{6}$ of the Earth's. That means that an object weighs less on the Moon that it does on Earth.

If an astronaut has a mass of 85kg…

his weight on Earth = 85kg x 10N/kg = **850N**

his weight on Moon = 85kg x $\frac{10}{6}$ N/kg = **141.7N**

13.3

What happens to the movement energy when things speed up or slow down?

When an object speeds up or slows down, its kinetic (movement) energy increases or decreases by transferring energy to or from the object. To understand this, you need to know...

- that work done equals energy transferred
- how work done, force and distance are related
- how mass and speed determine kinetic energy
- the result of friction against work done
- how to calculate kinetic energy.

Work

When a force moves an object, work is done on the object resulting in the transfer of energy. Energy is measured in **joules (J)**. Therefore…

$$\text{Work done (J)} = \text{Energy transferred (J)}$$

The relationship between work done, force and distance is shown by the following formula…

$$\text{Work done (J)} = \text{Force applied (N)} \times \text{Distance moved in direction of force (m)}$$

$$\frac{J}{N \times m}$$

Example

A man pushes a car with a steady force of 250N. The car moves a distance of 20m. How much work does the man do?

250N push →

Work done = Force applied x Distance moved
= 250N x 20m
= **5000J (or 5kJ)**

Work done against frictional forces is mainly transformed into heat energy. When work is done on an object that is able to change and recover its original shape, energy is stored in the object as elastic potential energy.

Kinetic Energy

Kinetic energy is the energy an object has because of its movement. It depends on two things: the **mass** of the object (kg) and the **speed** of the object (m/s).

Example

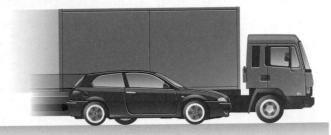

A moving car has kinetic energy as it has both mass and speed. As it moves with a greater speed, its mass is unchanged but it has more kinetic energy.

However, a moving truck has a greater mass than the car, so even if it is going slower than the car, it may have more kinetic energy.

HT Kinetic energy is calculated by this formula…

$$\text{Kinetic energy (J)} = \frac{1}{2} \times \text{Mass (kg)} \times \text{Speed}^2 \text{ (m/s)}^2$$

$$\frac{K.E.}{\frac{1}{2} \times m \times v^2}$$

Example

A car of mass 1000kg is moving at a speed of 10m/s. How much kinetic energy does it have?

Using the formula…

Kinetic energy = $\frac{1}{2}$ x Mass x Speed^2

= $\frac{1}{2}$ x 1000kg x (10m/s)^2

= **50 000J (or 50kJ)**

How Science Works

You need to be able to discuss the transformation of kinetic energy to other forms of energy in particular situations.

Example 1: Space Shuttles

When a space shuttle returns to Earth it has a lot of kinetic energy, i.e. it has a large mass and is travelling fast. As it enters the Earth's atmosphere, the shuttle encounters frictional forces and the kinetic energy is transformed into heat energy which slows it down.

The shuttle can reach extremely high temperatures because of the heat energy produced, which causes a risk of fire and explosion. Scientists have developed special heat shields to try to protect the body of space shuttles (and the astronauts in them) from this intense heat.

Example 2: Hydroelectricity

Hydroelectric power stations use the kinetic energy in moving water to produce electricity. A dam is built across a river valley and water builds up behind it. The water held behind the dam contains potential energy.

This potential energy is transformed to kinetic energy when the water is released down tubes inside the dam. The moving water is used to drive generators which transform the kinetic energy into electrical energy.

Example 3: Bungee Rides

A bungee ride consists of a spherical cage that is attached to two supporting arms by elastic cords. Just before the ride starts, the bungee cords are tightened which provides the elastic potential energy.

When the cage (attached to the cord) is released, the elastic potential energy contained in the cord is transformed to kinetic energy which propels the cage straight up into the air. The kinetic energy of the cage is reduced as it travels upwards (against the force of gravity, and due to air resistance) and the cord becomes stretched, so the remaining kinetic energy is transformed to elastic potential energy.

When the cord reaches the limit of its elasticity (at the top) the elastic potential energy is again transformed back into kinetic energy and the cage travels down towards the Earth again, assisted by gravity, but again, the force is reduced by air resistance. The kinetic energy is transformed back into elastic energy as the cord is stretched, until it reaches its limit of elasticity (which is less than the limit reached initially due to the energy that has been lost).

The elastic energy is transformed back into kinetic energy, the cage starts to move upwards again and the process is repeated with decreasing amounts of energy each time, until it is stopped.

13.4

What is momentum?

A moving object has momentum as well as kinetic energy. When looking at what happens to objects as a result of an explosion or collision, it is more useful to think in terms of momentum. To understand this, you need to know…

- how momentum, mass and velocity are related
- that momentum has both magnitude and direction
- what factors affect momentum
- how force, change in momentum and time taken for change are related (Higher Tier).

What is Momentum?

Momentum is a measure of the state of motion of an object. It is dependent upon two things:
- the mass of the object (kg)
- the velocity of the object (m/s) (see p.76).

A moving car has momentum as it has both mass and velocity. If the car moves with a greater velocity, it has more momentum providing its mass has not changed. However, a moving truck with a greater mass may have more momentum than the car even if its velocity is less.

The momentum of an object is calculated using the following formula:

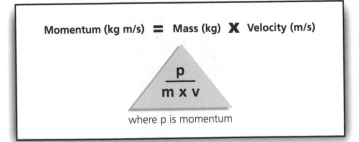

Momentum (kg m/s) = Mass (kg) X Velocity (m/s)

p

m X v

where p is momentum

Example 1

A car has a mass of 1200kg. It is travelling at a velocity of 30m/s. Calculate its momentum.

Using the formula…
momentum = Mass x Velocity
= 1200kg x 30m/s = **36 000kg m/s**

Example 2

A truck has a mass of 4000kg. Calculate its velocity if it has the same momentum as the car in Example 1.

Using the formula (rearranged using the formula triangle)…

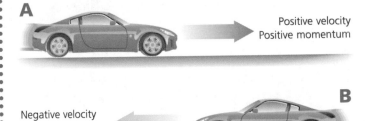

$$\text{Velocity} = \frac{\text{Momentum}}{\text{Mass}}$$

$$= \frac{36\,000\text{kg m/s}}{4000\text{kg}}$$

$$= \textbf{9m/s}$$

Since the truck has a greater mass than the car it can move at a slower speed and still have the same momentum.

Magnitude and Direction

Velocity and momentum are both quantities which have magnitude (size) and direction. The direction of movement is especially important when calculating momentum. For example…

If Car A (which is moving from left to right) has a positive velocity and, consequently, a positive momentum, then Car B (moving from right to left) will have a negative velocity and negative momentum because it is moving in the opposite direction to Car A.

A

Positive velocity
Positive momentum

Negative velocity
Negative momentum

B

Example

If car A has a mass of 1000kg and a velocity of 20m/s, then…
momentum = 1000kg x 20m/s
= **20 000kg m/s**

If car B has a mass of 1000kg and a velocity of -20m/s…
momentum = 1000kg x -20m/s
= **-20 000kg m/s**

Physics Unit 2

Force and Change in Momentum

When a force acts on a moving object, or a stationary object that is capable of moving, the object will experience a change in momentum.

An external force can…
- give a stationary object momentum (i.e. make it move)

- increase the momentum of a moving object
- decrease, or completely take away (i.e. stop), the momentum of a moving object.

The extent of the change in momentum depends on the size of the force and the length of time it is acting on the object.

HT Force, change in momentum and the time taken for the change are related by the following formula…

$$\text{Force (N)} = \frac{\text{Change in momentum (kg m/s)}}{\text{Time taken for change (s)}}$$

$$\frac{\Delta(mv)}{F \times t}$$

where $\Delta(mv)$ is change in momentum

The girl can increase the change in momentum of the ball, and, as a result, its velocity without increasing the force applied by 'following through' with her kick. Doing this will increase the time for which the force is applied. Some sports where following through increases the velocity of the ball are cricket, golf, tennis and squash.

Example

A girl kicks a stationary ball with a force of 30N. The force acts on the ball for 0.15 seconds. If the mass of the ball is 0.5kg, calculate…

a) the change in momentum of the ball and
b) the increase in velocity of the ball.

a) Rearranging the formula…

Change in momentum = Force x Time

= 30N x 0.15s

= **4.5kg m/s**

b) We can now work out the increase in velocity of the ball using the formula from page 87.

$$\text{Velocity} = \frac{\text{Momentum}}{\text{Mass}}$$

$$= \frac{4.5 \text{kg m/s}}{0.5 \text{kg}}$$

= **9m/s**

Collisions and Explosions

In any collision or explosion, the momentum in a particular direction after the event is the same as the momentum in that direction before the event, i.e. Momentum is **conserved,** provided that **no** external forces act.

Example 1

Two cars are travelling in the same direction along a road. Car A collides with the back of Car B and they stick together. Calculate their velocity after the collision.

Before

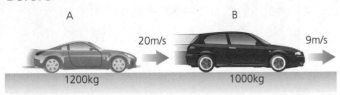

After

Momentum before collision...

= Momentum of A + Momentum of B
= (Mass x velocity of A) + (Mass x velocity of B)
= (1200kg x 20m/s) + (1000kg x 9m/s)
= 24 000kg m/s + 9000kg m/s
= 33 000kg m/s

Momentum after collision...

= Momentum of A and B stuck together
= (1200+1000) x v
= 2200v

Since momentum is conserved...

Total momentum before = Total momentum after
33 000 = 2200v

Therefore, $v = \frac{33\,000}{2200}$

= **15m/s**

Example 2

A gun fires a bullet of mass 0.01kg as shown below. The velocity of the bullet is 350m/s. Calculate the recoil velocity of the gun.

Before   **After**

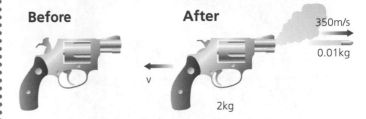

Firing a gun is an example of an explosion where the two objects, i.e. the gun and the bullet, move away from each other, rather than come towards each other as in a collision.

As we have seen, velocity and momentum are quantities that have magnitude and direction.

Since the gun and the bullet are moving in opposite directions, we will assume that the bullet has positive velocity and momentum which means that the gun has negative velocity and momentum.

Momentum before explosion = 0

(Neither the gun nor the bullet have momentum as they are not moving.)

Momentum after explosion...

= Momentum of bullet + Momentum of gun
= (Mass x velocity of bullet) + (Mass x velocity of gun)
= (0.01kg x 350m/s) + (2kg x -v)
= 3.5 – 2v

Since momentum is conserved...

Momentum after explosion = momentum before explosion
Momentum of bullet and momentum of gun = 0
(mass x velocity of bullet) + (mass x velocity of gun) = 0
(0.01kg x 350m/s) + (2kg x v) = 0
3.5 + 2v = 0
2v = -3.5
$v = \frac{-3.5}{2}$
v = **-1.75m/s**

Remember, the gun is moving in the opposite direction to the bullet so it has negative velocity.

How Science Works

You need to be able to use the ideas of momentum to explain safety features.

We already know that momentum is conserved in a collision (see p.89). This means that if a vehicle is brought to a sudden halt or makes a sudden change in direction, the people in the vehicle will continue with the same momentum as before. In other words, any people in the vehicle will continue to travel at the same speed and in the same direction as they were travelling immediately *before* the change.

Obviously, this can have fatal consequences, so cars have safety features to try to minimise injury and reduce the number of deaths.

Example 1: Seat Belts

Seat belts lock when a car crashes. They exert a force to counteract the momentum of the person wearing them. This prevents the wearer from flying through the windscreen or smashing against the inside of the car.

Cars travelling at faster speeds have greater momentum. This means that at high speeds the seatbelt has to exert a larger opposing force which can result in some bruising and injuries. However, the injuries caused by a seatbelt will be a lot less severe than those it prevents.

Example 2: Crumple Zones

A crumple zone is an area designed to 'crumple' on impact. This helps to increase the time over which the car changes momentum, i.e. instead of coming to an immediate halt there will be a few seconds during which the momentum is reduced. This means that the force exerted on the people inside the car will be reduced, which results in fewer injuries.

Example 3: Power-assisted steering and anti-lock braking systems (ABS)

These help the driver to control direction and speed, which can help to reduce change in momentum.

Example 4: Air bags

Air bags only partially inflate on impact so they are 'squashy'. They distribute the force of impact more evenly over the upper body area and reduce the momentum of the body more gradually.

13.5

What is static electricity, how can it be used and what is the connection between static electricity and electric currents?

Static electricity can be explained in terms of electrical charges; when electrical charges move they create an electric current.
To understand this, you need to know…
- how materials become electrically charged
- about repulsion and attraction
- how conductors are used
- how electrostatic charges are used.

Static Electricity

Some insulating materials can become electrically charged when they are rubbed against each other. The electrical charge (static) then stays on the material (i.e. it is not discharged).

You can generate static electricity by rubbing a balloon against a jumper. The electrically charged balloon will then attract very small objects.

Static builds up when electrons (which have a negative charge) are 'rubbed off' one material onto another. The material receiving the electrons becomes negatively charged and the one giving up electrons becomes positively charged.

For example, if you rub a perspex rod with a cloth, the perspex loses electrons to become positively charged. The cloth gains electrons to become negatively charged.

If you rub an ebonite rod with a fur, ebonite gains electrons to become negatively charged. Fur loses electrons to become positively charged.

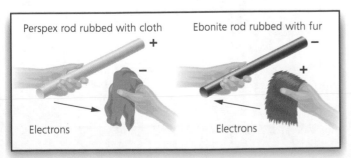

Perspex rod rubbed with cloth — Ebonite rod rubbed with fur

Electrons — Electrons

Repulsion and Attraction

When two charged materials are brought together, they exert a force on each other so they are attracted or repelled. Two materials with the same type of charge repel each other; two materials with different types of charge attract each other.

If you move a perspex rod near to a suspended perspex rod, the suspended perspex rod will be repelled.

If you move an ebonite rod near to a suspended perspex rod, the suspended perspex rod will be attracted.

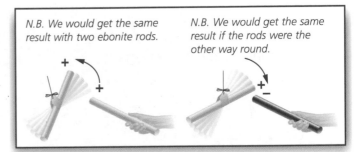

N.B. We would get the same result with two ebonite rods.

N.B. We would get the same result if the rods were the other way round.

The Uses of Static

Electrostatic charges can be very useful in industry and at home. They can be used in a variety of different ways, for example…
- reducing air pollution
- air fresheners
- photocopiers
- painting cars in the automobile industry.

Electrostatic Smoke Precipitator

Smoke precipitators are designed to remove solid smoke particles from waste gases before the gases are released into the environment.

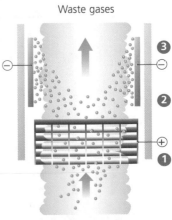

❶ Solid smoke particles become positively charged as they pass by a charged metal grid.

❷ These 'like' charges repel each other causing the particles to move away from the grid.

❸ The particles are then attracted to the collecting plates which are negatively charged, where they stick to form a layer of 'soot' which is regularly knocked loose.

Waste gases

Smoke and waste gases

The Uses of Static (cont.)

The Photocopier

An image of the page to be copied is projected onto an electrically charged plate (usually positively charged).

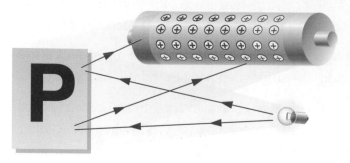

Light causes charge to leak away leaving an electrostatic impression of the page.

This charged impression on the plate attracts tiny specks of black powder, which is then transferred from the plate to paper. Heat is used to fix the final image on the paper.

Discharge of Static Electricity

A charged conductor (positive or negative) can be discharged, i.e. have any charge on it removed, by connecting it to Earth with a conductor.

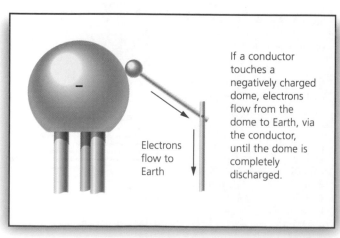

If a conductor touches a negatively charged dome, electrons flow from the dome to Earth, via the conductor, until the dome is completely discharged.

Electrons flow to Earth

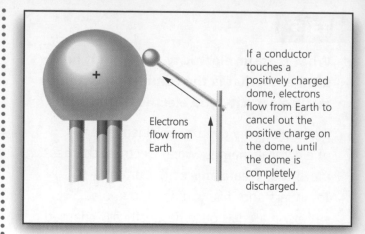

If a conductor touches a positively charged dome, electrons flow from Earth to cancel out the positive charge on the dome, until the dome is completely discharged.

Electrons flow from Earth

This flow of electrons through a solid conductor is an electric current. Metals conduct electricity well because electrons from their atoms can move freely throughout the metal structure.

HT The greater the charge on an isolated object, the greater the potential difference between the object and Earth.

If the potential difference between the object and a nearby earthed conductor becomes high enough, then this can cause the air molecules to ionise and there is a spark as discharge occurs.

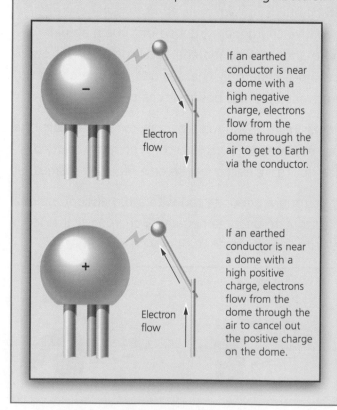

If an earthed conductor is near a dome with a high negative charge, electrons flow from the dome through the air to get to Earth via the conductor.

Electron flow

If an earthed conductor is near a dome with a high positive charge, electrons flow from the dome through the air to cancel out the positive charge on the dome.

Electron flow

How Science Works

You need to be able to explain why static electricity is dangerous in some situations and how precautions can be taken to ensure that the electrostatic charge is discharged safely.

Static electricity can create a spark or make people experience a mild electric shock when certain objects are touched. This is because certain materials, including dry human skin, can build up charges which then create a spark when something else is touched.

Although they can be slightly painful, these types of electric shocks are not dangerous or destructive. In some situations, however, static can be very hazardous and precautions need to be taken to ensure that it is safely discharged.

Example 1: Petrol Stations

When petrol is transferred either from a truck to the petrol station, or from the petrol pumps into our cars, a lot of friction is created. If a static charge is discharged in such an area, the results can be disastrous – a single spark could ignite the petrol vapours and cause an explosion. Therefore, when trucks transfer petrol into the petrol station, they use a grounding device on the hose that draws the electrical charges away from the petrol. This prevents any static sparks from occurring.

When filling a car with petrol you should...
- turn the engine off
- touch something metal when you get out of your car to get rid of any excess charges, e.g. from car seat materials
- avoid using mobile phones.
- place petrol containers on the ground when filling them up

Example 2: Refuelling Planes

During refuelling, the fuel gains electrons from the fuel pipe, making the pipe positively charged and the fuel negatively charged. The resulting voltage between the two can cause a spark (discharge). You can imagine what would happen next! To prevent this, either of the following can be done:
- earth the fuel tank with a copper conductor
- link the tanker and the plane with a copper conductor.

Example 3: Working on Computers

The internal electronics of a computer can be easily damaged by an electrical spark. To reduce the chance of this happening, technicians working on the inside of computers use a special pad on the floor and a grounded strap on their wrist. This takes any static charges away from their bodies before any damage can be done.

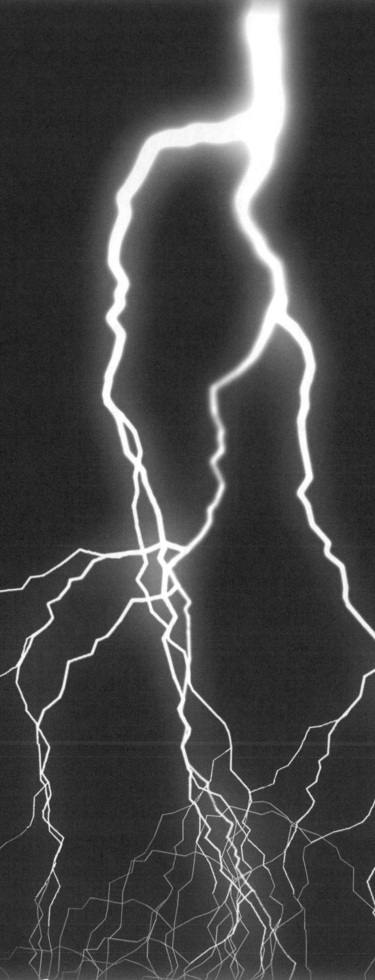

You need to be able to explain why static electricity is dangerous in some situations and how precautions can be taken to ensure that the electrostatic charge is discharged safely. (Continued from previous page).

Lightning and Buildings

During a thunderstorm, lightning bolts are attracted to the highest point in the area. Therefore, buildings can often be hit and damaged. To control the force of the electricity, lightning rods are attached to the top of a building (a rod is a piece of metal which runs from the very top of the building down to the ground). If lightning does then strike, it would hit the metal lightning rod (the highest part of the structure) and the current would flow down through the rod into the ground, where it would be safely discharged, with minimal damage to the building.

Lightning and People

Getting hit by lightning is rare but it can happen, and normally causes serious injury or death. However, there are some things you can do to reduce the chances of being hit:

- avoid holding anything metal as this can attract lightning – playing golf during a thunderstorm is not advised!
- try to be inside something that is grounded, e.g. a house or car. The inside of a car is normally fairly safe, as the rubber tyres will help to ground the electricity in the event of being hit.
- avoid standing under a tree during a storm – it might be the highest point in the area.

13.6

What does the current through an electrical circuit depend on?

The size of the push and the resistance determine the size of the current of the circuit. A supply tries to push a charge through a circuit and the circuit resists the charge. To understand this, you need to know...

- what affects the current in a circuit
- how potential difference, current and resistance are related
- which factors affect resistance
- what current–potential difference graphs show
- the differences between components connected in series and in parallel.

Circuits

An electric current will flow through an electrical component (or device) if there is a voltage or potential difference (p.d.) across the ends of the component.

In the following circuits, each cell and lamp are identical.

Circuit 1

Cell provides p.d. across the lamp. A current flows and the lamp lights up.

The amount of current that flows through the component depends on...

- the potential difference across the component
- the resistance of the component.

The Potential Difference Across the Component

The greater the potential difference or voltage across a component, the greater the current that flows through the component.

Circuit 2

Two cells together provide a bigger p.d. across the lamp. A bigger current now flows and the lamp lights up more brightly (compared to circuit 1).

The Resistance of the Component

Components resist the flow of current through them, i.e. they have **resistance** (measured in ohms). The greater the resistance of a component or components, the smaller the current that flows for a particular voltage, or the greater the voltage needed to maintain a particular current.

Circuit 3

Two lamps together have a greater resistance. A smaller current now flows and the lamps light up less brightly (compared to circuit 1).

Circuit 4

Two cells together provide a greater voltage. The same current as in circuit 1 will now flow. The lamps light up more brightly than in circuit 3 (the same as circuit 1).

Potential Difference and Current

The potential difference across a component in a circuit is measured in **volts (V)** using a **voltmeter** connected in **parallel** across the component.

The current flowing through a component in a circuit is measured in **amperes (A),** using an **ammeter** connected in **series.**

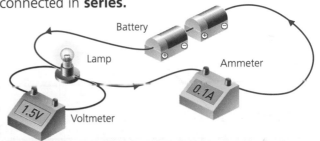

Battery

Lamp

Ammeter

0.1A

1.5V Voltmeter

Physics Unit 2

Resistance

Resistance is a measure of how hard it is to get a current through a component at a particular potential difference or voltage. Potential difference, current and resistance are related by the following formula:

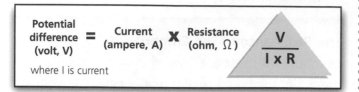

Potential difference (volt, V) = **Current (ampere, A)** x **Resistance (ohm, Ω)**

$$\frac{V}{I \times R}$$

where I is current

Example

Calculate the reading on the voltmeter in this circuit if the bulb has a resistance of 15 ohms.

0.2A

Use the formula...

Potential difference = current x resistance

= 0.2A x 15 Ω ← The reading on the ammeter is the current.

= **3V**

Resistance of Components

These can be investigated using the circuit above with a power pack instead of batteries. You can then draw **current–potential difference** graphs which show how the current through the component varies with the voltage across it.

Resistors

As long as the temperature of the resistor stays constant, the current through the resistor is directly proportional to the voltage across the resistor, regardless of which direction the current is flowing, i.e. if one doubles, the other also doubles.

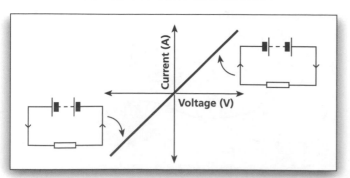

Filament Lamps

As the temperature of the filament increases and the bulb gets brighter then the resistance of the lamp increases, regardless of which direction the current is flowing.

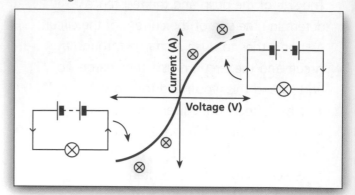

Diodes

A diode allows a current to flow through it in one direction only. It has a very high resistance in the reverse direction so no current flows.

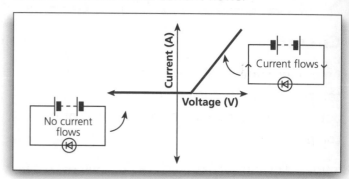

Light Dependent Resistor (LDR)

The resistance of an LDR depends on the amount of light falling on it. Its resistance decreases as the amount of light falling on it increases; this allows more current to flow.

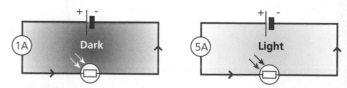

Thermistor

The resistance of a thermistor depends on its temperature. Its resistance decreases as the temperature of the thermistor increases; this allows more current to flow.

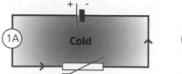

Series and Parallel Circuits

Components Connected in Series	**Components Connected in Parallel**
In a series circuit, all components are connected one after the other in one loop, going from one terminal of the battery to the other.	Components connected in parallel are connected separately in their own loop going from one terminal of the battery to the other.

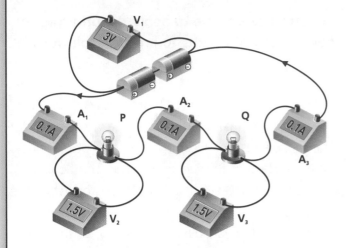

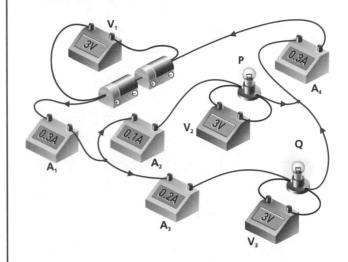

- The same current flows through each component, i.e. **$A_1 = A_2 = A_3$**. In the circuit above, each ammeter reading is 0.1A.
- The potential difference (or voltage) supplied by the battery is divided up between the components in the circuit, i.e. **$V_1 = V_2 + V_3$**. In the circuit above both bulbs have the same resistance so the voltage is divided equally. If one bulb had twice the resistance of the other, then the voltage would be divided differently, e.g. 2V and 1V.
- The total resistance is the sum of the individual resistances of the components, i.e. $\Omega = \Omega_p + \Omega_Q$. In the circuit above, if both P and Q each have a resistance of 15 ohms, the total resistance would be 15 ohms + 15 ohms = 30 ohms.

- The total current in the main circuit is equal to the sum of the currents through the separate components, i.e. **$A_1 = A_2 + A_3 = A_4$**. In the circuit above, 0.3A = 0.1A + 0.2A = 0.3A.
- The potential difference across each component is the same (and is equal to the p.d. of the battery) i.e. **$V_1 = V_2 = V_3$**. In the circuit above, each bulb has a p.d. of 3V across it.
- The amount of current which passes through a component depends on the resistance of the component. The greater the resistance, the smaller the current. In the circuit above, bulb P must have twice the resistance of bulb Q as only 0.1A passes through bulb P while 0.2A passes through bulb Q.

Connecting Cells in Series

The total potential difference provided by cells connected in series is the sum of the p.d. of each cell separately, providing that they have been connected in the same direction.

Each cell has a p.d. of 1.5V.

Total p.d. of battery
= 2 x 1.5V
= **3V**

Total p.d. of battery
= 3 x 1.5V
= **4.5V**

How Science Works

You should know the following standard symbols:

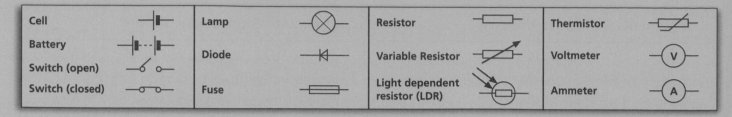

Cell	Lamp	Resistor	Thermistor
Battery	Diode	Variable Resistor	Voltmeter
Switch (open)		Light dependent resistor (LDR)	Ammeter
Switch (closed)	Fuse		

You need to be able to interpret and draw circuit diagrams using standard symbols.

Example 1

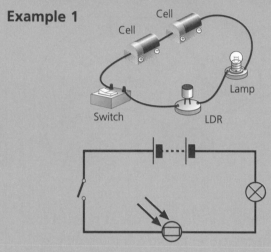

This is a series circuit. The light-dependent resistor is a variable resistor. When it is dark, it allows current through, but when more light falls on the sensor, its resistance increases and so less current is allowed through, making the light dimmer. This only happens when the switch is closed (which completes the circuit).

Example 2

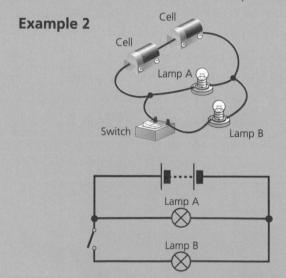

This is a parallel circuit. Lamp A will be on all the time, but lamp B will only come on when the switch is closed. Both lamps will be the same brightness.

You need to be able to apply the principles of basic electrical circuits to practical solutions.

Examples

In circuit 1, power from the battery flows through the gauge (on a car's dashboard) to a variable resistor. The variable resistor is controlled by a float that rides on the surface of the fuel in the tank. This float is always in contact with the variable resistor. When the fuel level is high, the float is high and so the resistance of the variable resistor is low. As the fuel level gets lower, the float gets lower and so the resistance of the variable resistor increases. The gauge on the dashboard inverts (reverses) the resistance of the variable resistor and displays it against a scale of E (empty) to F (full).

The low-fuel warning light is powered by a separate circuit (see circuit 2). Electricity flows from the battery through the light to a thermistor. A thermistor is like a switch. When it is submerged in fuel its resistance is very high; when it is in the air its resistance is very low. The thermistor is positioned near the bottom of the tank. When there is not much fuel left, the thermistor becomes exposed so its resistance falls to near zero. This allows current to flow through the circuit, which causes the light on the dashboard to light up.

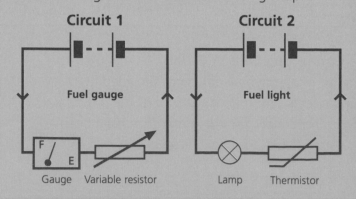

Circuit 1

Fuel gauge

Gauge   Variable resistor

Circuit 2

Fuel light

Lamp   Thermistor

13.7

What is mains electricity and how can it be used safely?

Although useful, mains electricity can be very dangerous so it is important to know how to use it safely. To understand this, you need to know...

- what a direct current is
- what an alternating current is
- how electrical appliances are connected to the mains
- the structure and wiring of a three-pin plug
- the use of a circuit breaker, fuse and the earth wire.

Currents

A **direct current** (d.c.) always flows in the same direction. Cells and batteries supply direct current.

An **alternating current** (a.c.) changes the direction of flow back and forth continuously. The number of complete cycles of reversal per second is called the **frequency**, and for UK mains electricity this is 50 cycles per second (Hertz).

In the UK, the mains supply has a voltage of about 230 volts which, if it is not used safely, can kill.

The 3-Pin Plug

Most electrical appliances are connected to the mains electricity supply using a cable and a 3-pin plug which is inserted into a socket on the ring main circuit.

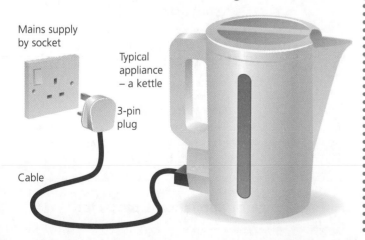

Mains supply by socket

Typical appliance – a kettle

3-pin plug

Cable

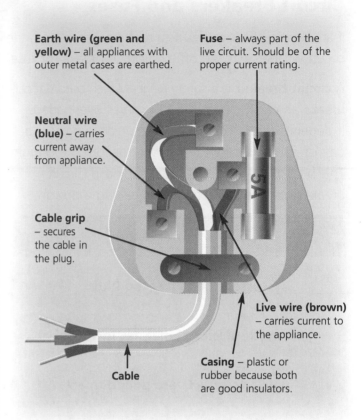

Earth wire (green and yellow) – all appliances with outer metal cases are earthed.

Fuse – always part of the live circuit. Should be of the proper current rating.

Neutral wire (blue) – carries current away from appliance.

Cable grip – secures the cable in the plug.

Cable

Live wire (brown) – carries current to the appliance.

Casing – plastic or rubber because both are good insulators.

5A

- The inner cores of the wires are made of copper because it is a good conductor.
- The outer layers are made of flexible plastic which is a good insulator.
- The pins of a plug are made from brass because it is a good conductor.

HT

The live terminal of the mains supply alternates between a positive and negative voltage with respect to the neutral terminal.

The neutral terminal stays at a voltage close to zero with respect to earth.

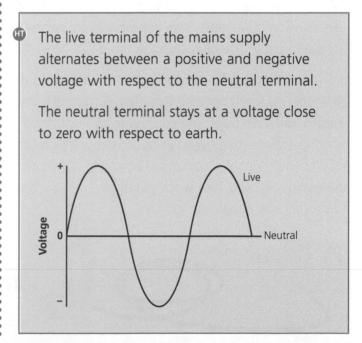

Voltage

Live

Neutral

0

+

–

Physics Unit 2

Circuit Breakers and Fuses

If an electrical fault causes a current that is too high, the circuit will be switched off by a circuit breaker or fuse.

A **circuit breaker** is a safety device which automatically breaks an electric circuit if it becomes overloaded. It depends on an electromagnet which separates a pair of contacts when the current becomes too high. This breaks the circuit (called 'tripping'). Circuit breakers can be easily reset by pressing a button.

A **fuse** is a short, thin piece of wire with a low melting point. When the current passing through it exceeds the current rating of the fuse, the fuse wire gets hot and melts or breaks, breaking the circuit. This prevents damage to the cable or the appliance that would be caused by overheating. The current rating of the fuse must be just above the normal working current of the appliance for the safety system to work properly.

A Circuit Breaker
current becomes too high
strength of electromagnet increases
pair of contacts are pulled apart
circuit is broken
cable or appliance is protected

A Fuse
current larger than current rating of fuse
fuse wire melts
circuit is broken
no current flows
cable or appliance is protected

Earthing

All electrical appliances with outer metal cases must be earthed. The outer case of an appliance is connected to the earth pin in the plug through the earth wire.

If a fault in the appliance connects the live wire to the case, the case will become **live.** The current will then 'run to earth' through the earth wire as this offers least resistance. This overload of current will cause the fuse to melt, or the circuit breaker to trip. Therefore, the earth wire and fuse work together to protect the appliance and user.

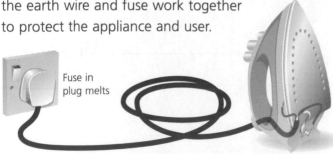

Fuse in plug melts

Earthing
Live Casing
short circuit
current surges to earth
fuse wire melts
circuit is broken
cable or appliance is protected

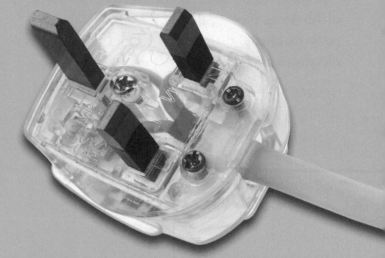

You need to be able to recognise errors in the wiring of a three-pin plug.

For safety reasons, it is very important that all plugs are wired correctly with no errors. Below are five examples of dangerously wired plugs.

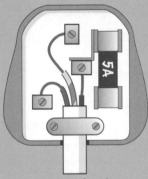

Bare wires showing

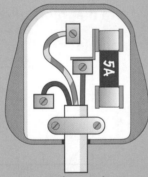

Live and neutral wrong way round

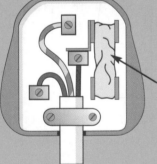

Silver foil

Proper fuse not installed

Earth wire not connected

Cable grip loose

You need to be able to recognise dangerous practices in the use of mains electricity.

Apart from making sure that all plugs are wired correctly, there are some common-sense practices which should be followed at all times:

- replace all broken plugs and frayed cables
- keep plugs and cables away from water or heat
- never overload a socket with too many plugs
- make sure your hands are dry when switching appliances on or off.

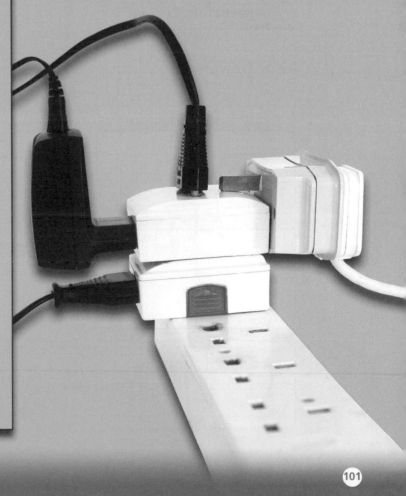

How Science Works

You need to be able to compare potential differences (voltage) of d.c. supplies and the peak potential differences of a.c. supplies from diagrams of oscilloscope traces.

Frequency and voltage can be compared using an oscilloscope.

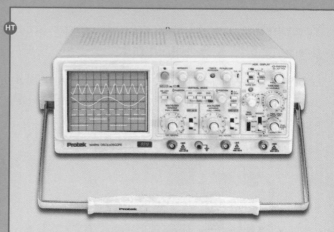

Direct Current

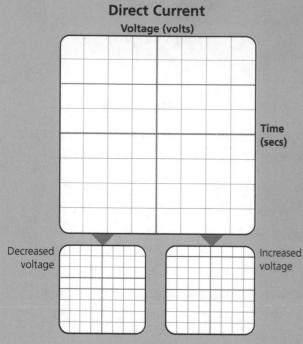

Voltage (volts)

Time (secs)

Decreased voltage

Increased voltage

Alternating Current

Decreased voltage (same frequency)

Increased voltage (same frequency)

Voltage (volts)

Time (secs)

Decreased frequency (same voltage)

Increased frequency (same voltage)

You need to be able to determine the period and hence the frequency of a supply from diagrams of oscilloscope traces.

Example

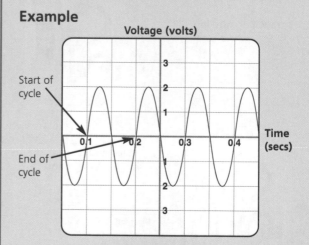

Voltage (volts)

Start of cycle

End of cycle

Time (secs)

The peak voltage is 2 volts and the frequency is 10 cycles per second, since one complete cycle takes 0.1 seconds.

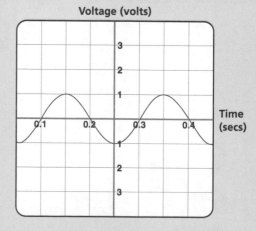

Voltage (volts)

Time (secs)

The peak voltage is 1 volt and the frequency is 5 cycles per second, since one complete cycle takes 0.2 seconds.

13.8

Why do we need to know the power of electrical appliances?

The power of an electrical appliance is the rate at which it transforms energy. If you know this and the potential difference, you can calculate the current and fuse needed for each appliance. To understand this, you need to know...

- what electric current is
- how to calculate power
- how power, potential difference and current are related
- the relationship between energy transformed, potential difference and charge
- how charge, current and time are related.

Power

An electric **current** is the flow of charge, which **transfers** electrical energy from a battery or power supply to components in a circuit. The rate of flow is measured in **amperes (A)**.

The components transform some of this electrical energy into other forms of energy, e.g. a resistor **transforms** electrical energy into heat energy. The rate at which energy is transformed in a device is called the **power**. This can be calculated using the formula...

$$\text{Power (watts, W)} = \frac{\text{Energy transformed (joule, J)}}{\text{Time (second, s)}}$$

Power can also be calculated using the formula...

$$\text{Power (watts, W)} = \text{Potential difference (volts, V)} \times \text{Current (amps, A)}$$

$$\frac{P}{V \times I}$$

where I is the current

HT Charge

The amount of electrical charge which passes any point in a circuit is measured in **coulombs (C)**. Charge can be calculated using the formula...

$$\text{Charge (coulomb, C)} = \text{Current (amps, A)} \times \text{Time (second, s)}$$

$$\frac{Q}{I \times T}$$

where Q is charge

Example

If the circuit below is switched on for 40 seconds and the current is 0.5 amps, what is the charge?

Using the formula...

Charge = Current x Time

= 0.5A x 40s = **20 coulombs**

Transforming Energy

As charge passes through a device, energy is transformed. The amount of energy transformed for every coulomb of charge depends on the size of the potential difference. The greater the potential difference, the more energy transformed per coulomb.

$$\text{Energy transformed (joule, J)} = \text{Potential difference (volt, V)} \times \text{Charge (coulomb, C)}$$

$$\frac{E}{V \times Q}$$

If the circuit alongside has a potential difference of 1.5V, how much energy is transformed?

Energy transformed = p.d. x Charge

= 1.5V x 20C

= **30 joules**

> The amount of electrical energy transformed by the bulb into light and heat energy

Remember, the charge gained this energy from the battery. It was transferred to the bulb in the 40 seconds the circuit was switched on.

How Science Works

You need to be able to calculate the current through an appliance from its power and the potential difference of the supply, and from this determine the size of the fuse needed.

When a new appliance is developed, the manufacturer needs to work out what size fuse it requires.

If the power and operating voltage (potential difference) are known, the current can be calculated by rearranging the power formula as follows:

$$\text{Current} = \frac{\text{Power}}{\text{Potential difference}}$$

Once the current has been calculated, the size of the fuse can then be determined. The fuse needs to be as close to the current as possible, but higher than it.

Fuses come in the following standard sizes: 1 amp, 3 amp, 7 amp, 13 amp, 20 amp, 25 amp and 30 amp.

Example

Device	Power	Voltage	Current	Ideal Fuse
Television	60W	230V	$\frac{60}{230}$ = 0.26A	3 amp
Oven	5500W	230V	$\frac{5500}{230}$ = 23.9A	25 amp
Computer	43W	16V	$\frac{43}{16}$ = 2.7A	3 amp
Drill	800W	240V	$\frac{800}{240}$ = 3.3A	5 amp
Microwave	1150W	230V	$\frac{1150}{230}$ = 5A	13 amp

13.9

What happens to radioactive substances when they decay?

We need to understand the structure of atoms in order to understand what happens to radioactive substances when they decay. To understand this, you need to know...

- the masses and relative charges of protons, neutrons and electrons
- what ions are
- what isotopes are
- what the mass number represents
- what effect alpha and beta decay have on radioactive nuclei
- the origins of background radiation.

Atoms

An atom is made up of three parts: protons, neutrons and electrons.

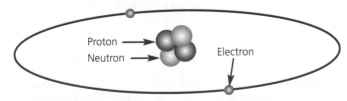

Atomic Particle	Relative Mass	Relative Charge
Proton	1	+1
Neutron	1	0
Electron	0 (nearly)	-1

An atom has the same number of protons as electrons so the atom as a whole has no electrical charge.

All atoms of a particular element have the same number of protons. Atoms of different elements have different numbers of protons. The number of protons defines the element.

The number of protons and neutrons in an atom is called its **mass number**. The total number of protons in an atom is called its **atomic number**.

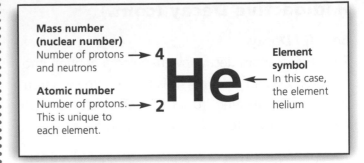

Mass number (nuclear number): Number of protons and neutrons → 4

Atomic number: Number of protons. This is unique to each element. → 2

Element symbol: In this case, the element helium

However, some atoms of the same element can have different numbers of neutrons. These are called **isotopes**.

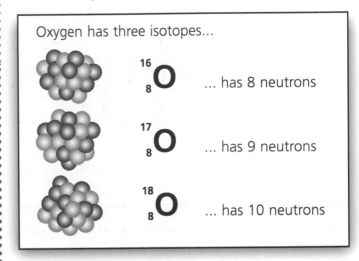

Oxygen has three isotopes...

$^{16}_{8}O$ ... has 8 neutrons

$^{17}_{8}O$ ... has 9 neutrons

$^{18}_{8}O$ ... has 10 neutrons

Radioactive Decay

Radioactive isotopes (radioisotopes or radionuclides) are atoms with unstable nuclei which may disintegrate and emit radiation. This is **radioactive decay** which results in the formation of a different atom with a different number of protons.

Alpha (α) Decay

The original atom decays by ejecting an alpha (α) particle from the nucleus. This particle is a helium nucleus: a particle made up of two protons and two neutrons. A new atom is formed with α decay.

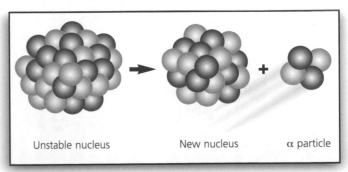

Unstable nucleus   New nucleus   α particle

Radioactive Decay (cont.)

Beta (β) Decay

The original atom decays by changing a neutron into a proton and an electron. This high energy electron which is now ejected from the nucleus is a beta (β) particle. A new atom is formed with β decay.

There is another type of radiation – gamma (γ) radiation. However, unlike alpha and beta, gamma emissions have no effect on the structure of the nucleus.

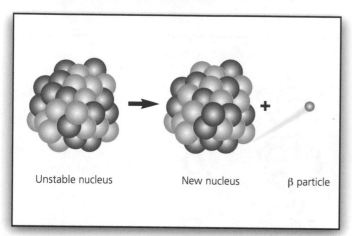

Unstable nucleus   New nucleus   β particle

Ionisation

When radioactive particles collide with neutral atoms or molecules they may become charged due to electrons being knocked out of their structure.

This alters their structure leaving them as charged particles called **ions**. Alpha and beta radiation are therefore known as ionising radiation and can damage molecules in healthy cells, which results in the death of the cell.

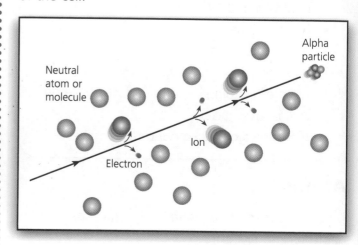

Neutral atom or molecule   Alpha particle   Ion   Electron

Background Radiation

Radiation occurs naturally all around us. This is known as background radiation. It only provides a very small dose altogether so there is no danger to our health.

13% of radiation is from man-made sources

87% of radiation is from natural sources

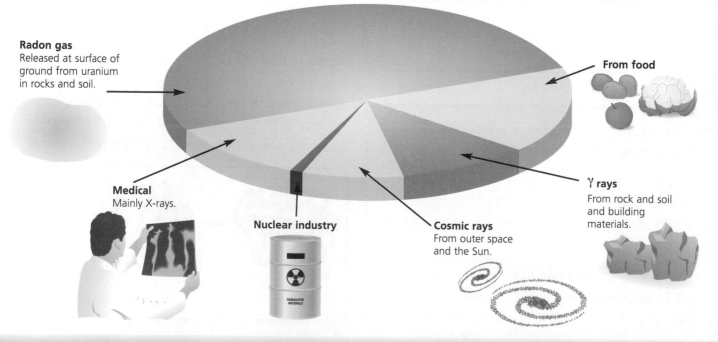

Radon gas
Released at surface of ground from uranium in rocks and soil.

Medical
Mainly X-rays.

Nuclear industry

Cosmic rays
From outer space and the Sun.

From food

γ rays
From rock and soil and building materials.

You need to be able to explain how the Rutherford and Marsden scattering experiment led to the 'plum pudding' model of the atom being replaced by the nuclear model.

In 1879, J.J. Thomson, a physicist, reasoned that since electrons were responsible for only a very small proportion of an atom's mass, they would take up an equally small proportion of an atom's size. He proposed that an atom consisted of a positive sphere of matter in which negative electrons were embedded.

The resulting model looked rather like a plum pudding, so it was known as the 'plum pudding' model of the atom. However, this model was disproved in 1911 by Ernest Rutherford, a British physicist, when he designed the gold foil scattering experiment.

Rutherford placed a thin piece of gold foil in the centre of a circular chamber lined with zinc sulfide. A radioactive source emitting alpha particles was focused on the gold foil target and the results were observed through a microscope.

Most alpha particles were seen to pass straight through the gold foil; this would indicate that the gold atoms were composed of large amounts of open space. However, some particles were deflected slightly and a few even bounced back towards the source. This would indicate that the alpha particles passed close to something positively charged within the atom and were repelled by it.

These observations brought Rutherford to conclude that...
- gold atoms, and therefore all atoms, consist largely of empty space with a small, dense positive core. He called this core the **nucleus**
- the nucleus is positively charged
- the electrons are arranged around the nucleus with a great deal of space between them.

This is called the **nuclear atomic model.**

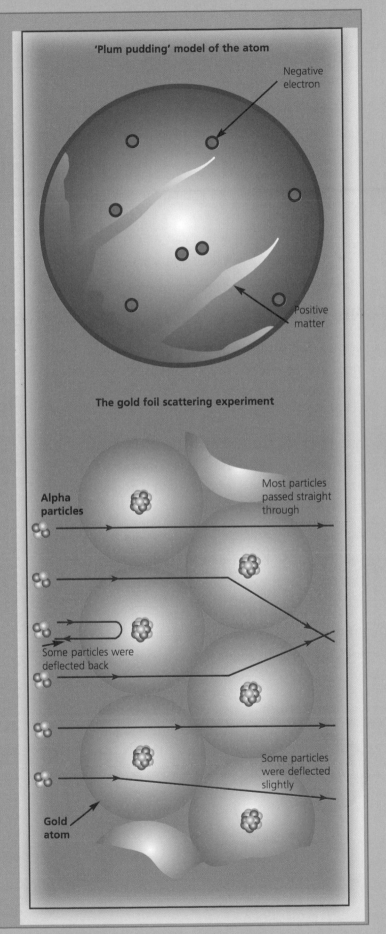

'Plum pudding' model of the atom

Negative electron

Positive matter

The gold foil scattering experiment

Alpha particles

Most particles passed straight through

Some particles were deflected back

Some particles were deflected slightly

Gold atom

Physics Unit 2

13.10

What are nuclear fission and nuclear fusion?

Nuclear fission is the splitting of atomic nuclei whilst nuclear fusion is the joining together of atomic nuclei. To understand this, you need to know...

- how uranium 235 and plutonium 239 are used
- how a chain reaction can be created
- how energy is released in stars.

Nuclear Fusion

Nuclear **fusion** is the **joining** together of two or more atomic nuclei to form a larger atomic nucleus. It takes a lot of energy – over 100 million Kelvin – to force the nuclei to fuse.

As a reaction, nuclear fusion generally releases more energy than it uses, which makes it self-sustaining, i.e. some of the energy produced is used to drive further fusion reactions.

This is how stars release energy. In the core of the Sun, hydrogen is converted to helium by fusion. This provides the energy to keep the Sun burning and allow life on Earth.

The fusion of two heavy forms of hydrogen (deuterium and tritium) is an example of nuclear fusion.

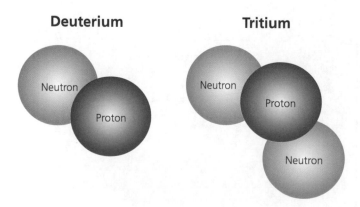

When they are forced together, the deuterium and tritium nuclei fuse together to form a new helium atom and an unchanged neutron.

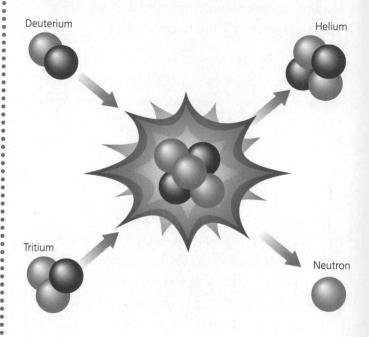

Nuclear Fission

Nuclear **fission** is the process of **splitting** atomic nuclei. It is used in nuclear reactors to produce energy to make electricity. The two substances commonly used are uranium 235 and plutonium 239.

The products of nuclear fission are radioactive and there are dangers with regard to the reaction getting out of control (e.g. Chernobyl). However, the amount of energy released by an atom during nuclear fission, or radioactive disintegration, is much greater than the energy released when a chemical bond is made between two atoms.

On a Small Scale
A uranium atom must first absorb a neutron before fission can take place. When a neutron collides with a very large nucleus (e.g. uranium) the nucleus splits up into two smaller nuclei (e.g. barium and krypton). This releases energy and new neutrons.

On a Large Scale
The new neutrons can each cause a new fission; this is a chain reaction (i.e. carries on and on and on...).

Small Scale Fission

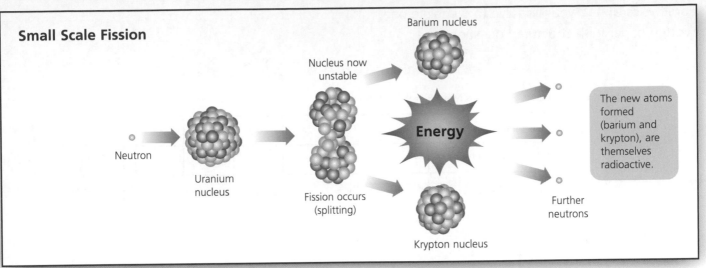

Barium nucleus

Nucleus now
unstable

Energy

Neutron

Uranium
nucleus

Fission occurs
(splitting)

Krypton nucleus

The new atoms
formed
(barium and
krypton), are
themselves
radioactive.

Further
neutrons

Large Scale Fission

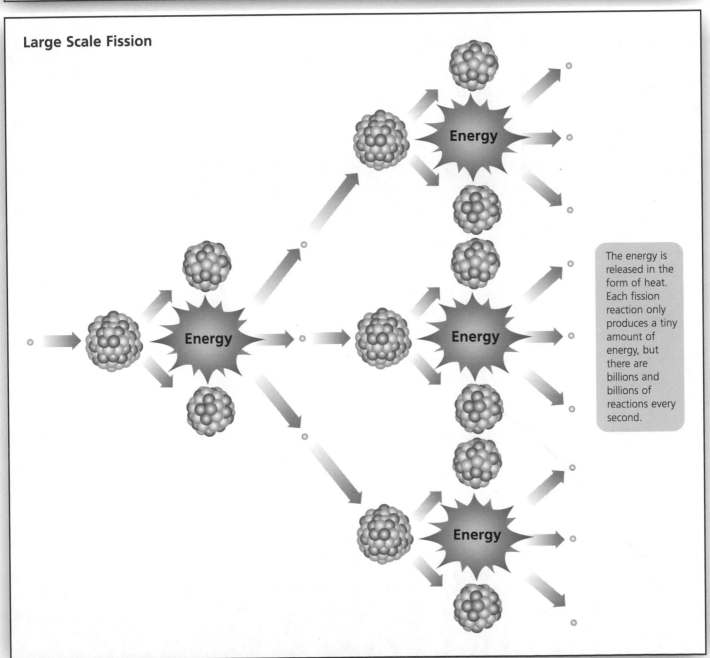

Energy

Energy

Energy

Energy

The energy is
released in the
form of heat.
Each fission
reaction only
produces a tiny
amount of
energy, but
there are
billions and
billions of
reactions every
second.

Example Questions

For Physics Unit 2, you will have to complete one
written paper with structured questions.

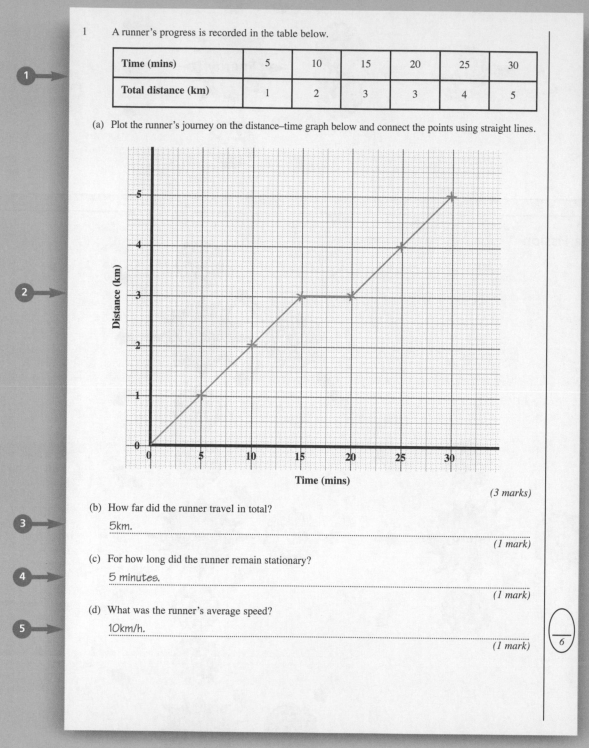

1   A runner's progress is recorded in the table below.

Time (mins)	5	10	15	20	25	30
Total distance (km)	1	2	3	3	4	5

(a)   Plot the runner's journey on the distance–time graph below and connect the points using straight lines.

(3 marks)

(b)   How far did the runner travel in total?

5km.

(1 mark)

(c)   For how long did the runner remain stationary?

5 minutes.

(1 mark)

(d)   What was the runner's average speed?

10km/h.

(1 mark)

6

1 Read the information carefully to make sure you understand what the data in a table shows before answering any questions.

2 Make sure you plot data accurately and neatly, otherwise you might get subsequent questions wrong!

3 Don't forget to include units (e.g. km) in your answers.

4 In a distance–time graph, a flat horizontal line means the object is not moving.

5 Average speed = $\dfrac{\text{Distance (km)}}{\text{Time (hours)}} = \dfrac{5}{0.5} = 10$km/h

Key Words

Acceleration – the rate at which a body increases in speed

Alternating current (a.c.) – an electric current which changes direction of flow continuously

Attraction – the drawing together of two materials with different types of charges

Charged – having an overall positive or negative electric charge

Circuit breaker – a safety device which breaks an electric circuit automatically when it becomes overloaded

Current – the rate of flow of an electrical charge, measured in amperes (A)

Diode – an electrical device that allows current to flow in one direction

Direct current (d.c.) – an electric current which flows in one direction

Distance – the space between two points

Distance–time graph – represents speed (distance travelled against time taken)

Electron – a negatively charged subatomic particle

Electrostatic – producing or caused by static electricity

Energy – the capacity of a physical system to do work; measured in joules (J)

Force – a push or pull acting upon an object

Friction – the resistive force between two surfaces as they move over each other

Fuse – a thin piece of metal which overheats and melts to break an electric circuit if it is overloaded

Ion – a charged particle formed when an atom gains or loses electrons

Isotopes – atoms of the same element but with a different number of neutrons

Joule – a measure of energy and work done

Kinetic energy – the energy possessed by a body due to its movement

Mass – the quantity of matter in a body

Momentum – a measure of the state of motion of a body as a product of its mass and velocity

Newton – a measure of force

Neutron – a neutrally charged subatomic particle

Nuclear fission – the splitting of atomic nuclei

Nuclear fusion – the joining together of atomic nuclei

Parallel circuit – a circuit where there are two (or more) paths for the current to take

Potential difference (p.d.) / voltage – the difference in electrical charge between two charged points

Proton – a positively charged subatomic particle

Repulsion – the pushing away of two materials with the same type of charge

Resistance – opposition to the flow of an electric current

Resistor – an electrical device that resists the flow of an electric current

Series circuit – a circuit where there is one path for the current to take

Speed – the rate at which a body moves

Static electricity – electricity produced by friction

Terminal velocity – the maximum velocity reached by a falling body (gravitational force is equal to the frictional forces acting on it)

Thermistor – a resistor whose resistance varies greatly with temperature

Transfer – to move energy from one place to another

Transform – to change energy from one form into another, e.g. electrical energy to heat energy

Velocity – the speed at which a body moves in a particular direction

Velocity–time graph – represents acceleration (velocity against time taken)

Voltage / potential difference (p.d.) – the difference in electrical charge between two charged points

Weight – the gravitational force exerted upon a body

Work – the energy transfer that occurs when a force causes a body to move a certain distance

Index and Acknowledgements

Index

A

Acceleration 77, 82
Aerobic respiration 24
Alkali metals 43
Alleles 33-35, 39
Alpha particles 105
Alternating current (a.c.) 99
Ammonia 65
Atom economy 55, 57
Atomic number 42, 50
Atoms 105

B

Beta particles 106
Bile 25
Biomass 18-19
Blood glucose 27, 29-30
Body temperature 28

C

Carbon cycle 22
Catalysts 59, 62
Cells 12-13
Charge 103
Chromosomes 31-35
Circuit breakers 100
Circuits 95-98, 100
Components (electrical) 96-98
Compounds 43
Covalent bonds 45
Current 95, 99
Cystic fibrosis 35
Cytoplasm 12

D

Diabetes 27, 29-30
Differentiation 35
Diffusion 14
Direct current (d.c.) 99, 102
Distance-time graphs 76, 78-79
DNA 31

E

Earth (electrical) 100
Electrolysis 67-69, 72
Electronic structure 43
Electrons 42
Embryo screening 38
Empirical formulae 52
Endothermic reactions 63
Energy 15, 18-20, 85-86, 103
Enzymes 23-26
Exothermic reactions 63

F

Fertilisation 32
Food chains 18-20
Food production 19, 21
Forces 80-90
Friction 80
Fuses 100, 104

G

Gametes 31
Gaseous reactions 64
Genes 33-39
Genetic disorders 35
Genetics 31-39
Giant structures 46

H

Haber process 56, 64
Halogens 43
Huntington's disease 35

I

Indicators 69
Industrial processes 57, 66
Inheritance 33-34
Ion content (of body) 27
Ionic bonds 44
Ionisation 106
Isotopes 50, 105

K

Kinetic energy 85-86

M

Mass number 50
Meiosis 32
Mendel, Gregor 36
Metals 46
Minerals 16
Mitochondria 12
Mitosis 32
Mixtures 43
Mole (mol) 53
Momentum 87-90
Movement 80

N

Nanomaterials 47, 49
Neutralisation 70
Neutrons 42
Nuclear fission 108-109
Nuclear fusion 108-109

O

Osmosis 15

P

Percentage mass 52
Percentage yield 55
pH scale 69
Photosynthesis 15-17
Plug (3-pin) 99, 101
Plum pudding model 107
Potential difference 95, 102
Power 103-104
Protons 42
Pyramids of biomass 18-20

R

Radiation 105-106
Radioactive decay 105
Rate of reaction 58-66
Redox reactions 67
Relative atomic mass 51
Relative formula mass 51, 57
Resistance 95
Reversible reactions 56, 64

S

Salts (of metals) 70-71, 73
Simple molecular compounds 43
Speed 76
State symbols 67
Static electricity 91-94
Stem cells 35, 37
Stopping distance 80

Subatomic particles 42, 50, 105
Sustainable development 65

V

Velocity 76-79, 83-84, 87
    Terminal 83-84
Velocity–time graphs 77-79, 84
Voltage 95

W

Waste products 28
Work 85

Acknowledgements

The author and publisher would like to thank everyone who has contributed to this book:

IFC   ©iStockphoto.com / Andrei Tchernov
p.3   ©iStockphoto.com / Andrei Tchernov
p.5   ©iStockphoto.com / Audrey Roorda
p.6   ©iStockphoto.com / Todd Smith
p.7   ©iStockphoto.com / James Antrim
p.17   ©iStockphoto.com / Ståle Edstrøm
p.21   ©iStockphoto.com / Matthew Scherf
p.30   ©iStockphoto.com / Diane Diederich
p.30   ©iStockphoto.com / Radu Razvan
p.37   ©iStockphoto.com / Andrei Tchernov
p.37   ©iStockphoto.com / Gary Caviness
p.38   ©iStockphoto.com
p.57   ©iStockphoto.com / Jean Schweitzer
p.61   ©iStockphoto.com / Viktor Pryymachuk
p.61   ©iStockphoto.com / Mark Evans
p.66   ©iStockphoto.com / Jon Kroninger
p.79   ©iStockphoto.com / Nigel Silcock
p.86   ©iStockphoto.com / Stijn Peeters
p.90   ©iStockphoto.com / Linda Shannon
p.90   ©iStockphoto.com / Peter van Leyen
p.90   ©iStockphoto.com / Antonio Ovejero Diaz
p.93   ©iStockphoto.com / Benson Trent
p.93   ©iStockphoto.com / Christoph Ermel
p.93   ©iStockphoto.com / Andrew Howe
p.94   ©iStockphoto.com / Glenn Slingsby
p.94   ©iStockphoto.com / Luis Carlos Torres
p.94   ©iStockphoto.com / Gilles Glod
p.101 ©iStockphoto.com / Paul Cowan
p.104 ©iStockphoto.com / Sim Kay Seng

Project Editor: Rebecca Skinner
Editors: Charlotte Christensen, Rachael Hemsley and Katie Smith
Cover and Concept Design: Sarah Duxbury
Designers: Richard Arundale, Anne-Marie Taylor and Ian Wrigley
Artwork: HL Studios

ISBN 978-1-905129-65-2

Published by Lonsdale, a division of Huveaux Plc.

This revision and classroom companion is matched to the new single award **AQA GCSE Additional Science** specification. It builds on the scientific explanations and concepts covered *AQA GCSE Science Revision and Classroom Companion*, also published by Lonsdale, providing full coverage of the three units of substantive content (**Biology 2**, **Chemistry 2** and **Physics 2**) and the procedural content, **How Science Works**, which is explained thoroughly on pages 4–11.

For each sub-section of substantive content, the AQA specification identifies **activities** you should be able to complete using your skills, knowledge and understanding of how science works. Many of these activities focus on social-science issues, and require you to evaluate information, develop arguments and draw conclusions. These activities are dealt with on the How Science Works pages, which are integrated into the three main units.

How to use this book

This revision and classroom companion focuses on the **externally assessed material** on the specification. It does not cover the investigative skills assignment and practical skills assessment.

> **HT** It is suitable for use by **Foundation and Higher Tier** students. Any material that is limited to the Higher Tier exam papers is clearly labelled and appears within a grey box.

The **contents list** and **page headers** clearly identify the separate units, to help you revise for the individual exam papers.

All of the exam papers will include questions on **How Science Works**, so make sure you work through the How Science Works section at the front of this guide and the dedicated pages in the relevant unit. The points identified on the How Science Works pages are designed to provide a starting point, from which you can begin to develop your own conclusions. They are not meant to be definitive or prescriptive.

You will find **exam-style questions**, along with model answers and handy hints at the end of each unit. There is also a page of **key words** and definitions for each unit. These pages can be used as checklists to help you with your revision. Make sure you are familiar with all the words listed and understand their meanings and relevance - they are central to your understanding of the material in that unit!

Author Information

Andrew Catterall (Physics), Lynn Henfield (Biology) and Christine Horbury (Chemistry) are all science consultants for LEAs. They work closely with the exam boards and have an excellent understanding of the new science specifications, which they are helping to implement in local schools.

As former science teachers, with over 70 years experience between them, their main objective in writing this book was to produce a user-friendly revision guide for students, which would also provide a useful reference for teachers. As such, this guide provides full coverage of all the essential material, cross-referenced to the specification for ease of use and presented in a clear and interesting manner that is accessible to everyone.

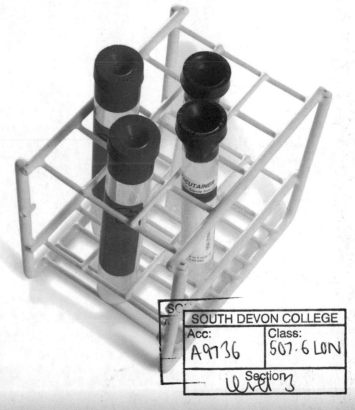

Contents